— Great Themes of the Bible —

CREATION:

Living in and as God's Creation

ABINGDON PRESS

NASHVILLE

GREAT THEMES OF THE BIBLE
Creation: Living in and as God's Creation

Copyright © 2006 by Abingdon Press

ISBN 0-687-34343-7

This book is printed on recycled, acid-free, and elemental-chlorine–free paper.

MANUFACTURED IN THE UNITED STATES OF AMERICA

06 07 08 09 10 11 12 13 14 15—10 9 8 7 6 5 4 3 2 1

Table of Contents

Welcome to *Great Themes of the Bible* 4

Using the Books in *Great Themes of the Bible* 8

Organizing a *Great Themes of the Bible* Small Group 10

Leading a *Great Themes of the Bible* Small Group 12

Introducing the Great Theme 15

SESSION 1
God Cares for All Creation 19

SESSION 2
We Praise God Who Created and Knows Us 29

SESSION 3
God Cares When All Seems Hopeless 39

SESSION 4
God Offers Life and Hope 49

SESSION 5
God Offers Meaning and Peace in Jesus Christ 57

SESSION 6
Trust in God Leads to True Wisdom 67

SESSION 7
The Path of Integrity 77

Appendix 86

Welcome to
Great Themes of the Bible

We are pleased that you have chosen *Great Themes of the Bible* for your small-group study. This series of study books cultivates faith formation in contemporary life using reliable principles of Christian education to explore major themes of the Bible, the issues and questions generated by these themes, and how the Bible illuminates our response to them in daily life. The sessions provide many opportunities for spiritual growth through worship, study, reflection, and interaction with other participants.

Great Themes of the Bible Cultivates Faith Formation in Contemporary Life

Who is God? How is God at work in our world? How does God call us and relate to us? How do we relate to God and to one another? What does Jesus Christ reveal to us about God? What is the potential for life in which we choose to be committed to God through Jesus Christ? How do we find hope? Such questions are at the heart of faith formation in contemporary life.

The Bible presents great themes that are universally relevant for the faith formation of all human beings in all times and places. Great themes such as call, creation, covenant, Christ, commitment, and community provide points of encounter between contemporary life and the times, places, and people in the Bible. As we reflect upon faith issues in our daily lives, we can engage biblical themes in order to learn more about God and in order to interpret what it means to live with faith in God.

The great themes of the Bible are the great themes of life. They generate questions and issues today just as they did for those in the biblical world. As we identify and explore these themes, we also engage the related questions and issues as they emerge in our contemporary life and culture. Exploring the Bible helps us see how people in the biblical world dealt with the issues and questions generated by a particular theme. Sometimes they responded exactly the way we would respond. Other times, they responded quite differently. In every case, however, we can glimpse God at work as we compare and contrast their situations with our own.

In Christian faith formation, we delve again and again into the Bible as we reflect upon our daily lives in light of Christian teaching. One way to imagine this process is by envisioning a spiral. A theme in the Bible generates questions and issues. We reflect upon the theme and consider the questions and issues it raises in our contemporary lives. We read the Bible and ask ourselves how the stories and teachings inform the theme and its questions and issues. We reflect upon the insights we have gained and perhaps make adjustments in our lives. We spiral through a particular theme and its issues and questions more than once as we look to the Bible for help, guidance, and hope. As we participate in this ongoing process, we gain deeper awareness of who God is and what God wants us to do, to be, and to become. The books in the *Great Themes of the Bible* series are structured around this spiraling process of faith formation.

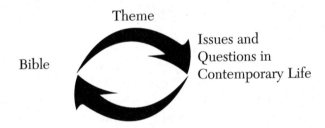

Theme

Bible

Issues and
Questions in
Contemporary Life

Great Themes of the Bible Is Built Upon Reliable Christian Education Principles

The sessions in each of the books in *Great Themes Of The Bible* are based on the Scriptures and lesson guides in the *Uniform Series of International Bible Lessons for Christian Teaching*. These guides provide reliable Christian education principles to those who write the books. Session development for a book in *Great Themes of the Bible* is guided by a unifying principle that illuminates the unity between life and the Bible by emphasizing a key theme. The principle contains three components: a life statement, a life question, and a biblical response.

The lesson guides in the Uniform Series also include statements for every Scripture that help the writer to think about and develop the sessions. These statements occur in five categories or matrices: Learner, Scripture, Faith Interaction, Teaching Strategies, and Special Interest.

Statements in the Learner matrix identify general characteristics describing life stages, developmental issues, and particular experiences (special needs, concerns, or celebrations) that characterize learners.

Statements in the Scripture matrix identify a variety of key issues, questions, practices, and affirmations raised from the biblical texts. These may include historical, cultural, ethical, and theological perspectives.

Statements in the Faith Interaction matrix identify ways in which learners and Scripture might interact in the context of the Bible study. The statements relate to personal, communal, and societal expressions of faith.

Statements in the Teaching Strategies matrix suggest ways for writers to create sessions that connect Scripture and learners through a variety of educational methods that take into account the different ways people learn.

Statements in the Special Interest matrix identify ways writers might address topics of special concern that are particularly appropriate to the Scripture text: handicapping conditions, racial and ethnic issues, drug and alcohol abuse, and ecology, for example.

While the Faith Interaction matrix provides the beginning point for each session in a book in the *Great Themes of the Bible,* learning goals employed by the writers arise from all these matrices.

Great Themes of the Bible Provides Opportunities for Spiritual Growth

The books in *Great Themes of The Bible* offer you an opportunity to see the vital connection between daily life and the Bible. Every session begins and ends with worship in order to help you experience God's presence as you participate in the sessions. The small group sessions also provide opportunities to develop friendships with others that are based upon respect, trust, and mutual encouragement in faith formation.

The following principles guide our approach to spiritual growth and faith formation:

- Faith and life belong together. We seek to discover connections or crossing points between what God reveals in the Bible and the needs, choices, and celebrations of our ordinary experience. Biblical themes provide this crossing point.
- Everyone is a theologian. *Theology* may be defined as "loving God with our minds" as well as with our hearts. All in your group, regardless of background, are fully qualified to do that.
- Adults learn best through reflection on experience. No longer are we blank tablets on which new knowledge must be imprinted. We can draw on a fund of experiences and ask what it means for us in light of Scripture and Christian teaching about God and creation.
- Questions stimulate spiritual growth more than answers. An authoritative answer seems final and discourages further thinking, while a stimulating question invites further creative exploration and dialogue.
- Learning involves change, choice, and pain. If we are to take seriously what God is telling us in Scripture, we must be open to changing our opinions, making new lifestyle choices, and experiencing the pain of letting go of the old and moving into a new and unknown future, following the God of continuing creation.
- Community sharing fosters spiritual growth. When a group commits to struggling together with questions of faith and life, they share personal experiences, challenge assumptions, deepen relationships, and pray. God's Spirit is present. The God of continuing creation is at work.

We pray that you will experience the freedom to ask questions as you explore the great themes in your life and in the Bible. We pray that you will encounter and experience the life-transforming love of God as you become part of a *Great Themes of the Bible* group. And finally, we pray that you will see yourself as a beloved human being created in the image of God and that you will grow in your love of God, self, and neighbor.

Using the Books in
Great Themes of the Bible

Each book in the *Great Themes of the Bible* series has within its pages all you need to lead or to participate in a group.

At the beginning of each book you will find:

- suggestions for organizing a *Great Themes of the Bible* small group.
- suggestions for different ways to use the book.
- suggestions for leading a group.
- an introduction to the great theme of the Bible that is at the center of all the sessions.

In each of the seven sessions you will find:

- a focus statement that illuminates the particular issues and questions of the theme in contemporary life and in the Scriptures for the session.
- opening and closing worship experiences related to the focus of each session.
- concise, easy-to-use leader/learner helps placed in boxes near the main text to which they refer.
- main content rich with illustrations from contemporary life and reliable information about the Scriptures in each session.

In the Appendix you will find:

- a list of Scriptures that illuminate the biblical theme.
- information about The Committee on the Uniform Series.

Books in the *Great Themes of the Bible* series are designed for versatility of use in a variety of settings.

Small Groups on Sunday Morning. Sunday morning groups usually meet for 45 minutes to an hour. If your group would like to go into greater depth, you can divide the sessions and do the study for longer than seven weeks.

Weekday or Weeknight Groups. We recommend 60 to 90 minutes for weekday/weeknight groups. Participants should prepare ahead by reading the content of the session and choosing one activity for deeper reflection and study. A group leader may wish to assign these activities.

A Weekend Retreat. For a weekend retreat, distribute books at least two weeks in advance. Locate and provide additional media resources and reference materials, such as hymnals, Bibles, Bible dictionaries and commentaries, and other books. If possible, have a computer with Internet capabilities on site. Tell participants to read their study books before the retreat. Begin on Friday with an evening meal or refreshments followed by gathering time and worship. Review the introduction to the theme. Do the activities in Session 1. Cover Sessions 2, 3, 4, 5, and 6 on Saturday. Develop a schedule that includes time for breaks, meals, and personal reflection of various topics and Scriptures in the sessions. Cover Session 7 on Sunday. End the retreat with closing worship on Sunday afternoon.

Individual Devotion and Reflection. While the books are designed for small-group study, they can also be beneficial for individual devotion and reflection. Use the book as a personal Bible study resource. Read the Scriptures, then read the main content of the sessions. Adapt the questions in the leader/learner boxes to help you reflect upon the issues related to the biblical theme. Learning with a small group of persons offers certain advantages over studying alone. In a small group, you will encounter people whose life experiences, education, opinions and ideas, personalities, skills, talents, and interests may be different from yours. Such differences can make the experience of Bible study richer and more challenging.

Organizing a *Great Themes of the Bible* Small Group

Great Themes of the Bible is an excellent resource for all people who are looking for meaning in their daily lives, who want to grow in their faith, and who want to read and reflect upon major themes in the Bible. They may be persons who are not part of a faith community yet who are seekers on a profound spiritual journey. They may be new Christians or new members who want to know more about Christian faith. Or they may be people who have been in church a long time but who feel a need for spiritual renewal. All such persons desire to engage more deeply with issues of faith and with the Bible in order to find meaning and hope.

Great Themes of the Bible is an excellent small-group study for those who have completed *Beginnings,* a program that introduces the basics of Christian faith. It is ideal for those who are not yet involved in an ongoing Bible study, such as *Adult Bible Studies,* DISCIPLE, *Genesis to Revelation,* and *Journey Through the Bible,* or for those who prefer short-term rather than long-term studies. *Great Themes of the Bible* also provides a point of entry for those who have never been involved in any kind of Bible study.

Starting a *Great Themes of the Bible* study group is an effective way to involve newcomers in the life of your local church. If you want to start a *Great Themes of the Bible* small group as part of the evangelism program in your local church, follow the steps below.

- Read through the *Great Themes of the Bible* study book. Think about the theme, the issues generated by the theme, and the Scriptures. Prepare to respond to questions that someone may ask about the study.

- Develop a list of potential participants. An ideal size for a small group is 7 to 12 people. Your list should have about twice your target number (14 to 24 people). Have your local church purchase a copy of the study book for each of the persons on your list.

- Decide on a location and time for your *Great Themes of the Bible* group. Of course, the details can be negotiated with those persons who accept the invitation; but you need to sound definitive and clear to prospective group members. "We will initially set Wednesday night from 7 to 9 P.M. at my house for our meeting time" will sound more attractive than "Well, I don't know when or where we would be meeting; but I hope you will consider joining us."

- Identify someone who is willing to go with you to visit the persons on your list. Make it your goal to become acquainted with each person you visit. Tell them about *Great Themes of the Bible*. Give them a copy of the study book for this group. Even if they choose not to attend the small group at this time, they will have an opportunity to read the book on their own. Tell each person the initial meeting time and location and how many weeks the group will meet. Invite them to become part of the group. Thank them for their time.

- Publicize the new *Great Themes of the Bible* study through as many channels as are available. Announce it during worship. Print notices in the church newsletter and bulletin and on the church Web site if you have one. Use free public event notices in community newspapers. Create flyers for mailing and posting in public places.

- A few days before the session begins, give a friendly phone call or send an e-mail to thank all persons you visited for their consideration and interest. Remind them of the time and location of the first meeting.

For more detailed instructions about starting and maintaining a small group, read *How to Start and Sustain a Faith-based Small Group,* by John D. Schroeder (Abingdon, 2003).

Leading a *Great Themes of the Bible* Small Group

A group may have one leader for all the sessions, or leadership may be rotated among the participants. Leaders do not need to be experts in Bible study because the role of the leader is to facilitate discussion rather than to impart information or teach a particular content. Leader and learner use the same book and share the same commitment to read and prepare for the *Great Themes of the Bible* session each week. So what does the leader actually do?

A Leader Prepares for the Session

Pray. Ask for God's guidance as you prepare to lead the session.

Read. Read the session and its Scriptures ahead of time. Jot down questions or insights that occur during the reading. Look at the leader/learner helps in the boxes.

Think about group participants. Who are they? What life issues or questions might they have about the theme? about the Scriptures?

Prepare the learning area. Gather any needed supplies, such as sheets of newsprint, markers, paper and pencils, Bibles, hymnals, audio-visual equipment, masking tape, a Bible dictionary, Bible commentaries, and a Bible atlas. If you are meeting in a classroom setting, arrange the chairs in a circle or around a table. Make sure that everyone will have a place to sit.

Prepare a worship center. Find a small table. Cover it with an attractive cloth. Place a candle in a candleholder on the center. Place matches nearby to light the candle. Place on the worship center a Bible or other items that relate to or illuminate the session focus.

Pray. Before the participants arrive, pray for each one. Ask for God's blessing on your session. Offer thanks to God for the opportunity to lead the session.

A Leader Creates a Welcoming Atmosphere

Hospitality is a spiritual discipline. A leader helps create an environment that makes others feel welcome and that helps every participant experience the freedom to ask questions and to state opinions. Such an atmosphere is based upon mutual respect.

Greet participants as they arrive. Say their names. If the group is meeting for the first time, use nametags.

Listen. As group discussion unfolds, affirm the comments and ideas of participants. Avoid the temptation to dominate conversation or "correct" the ideas of other participants.

Affirm. Thank people for telling about what they think or feel. Acknowledge their contributions to discussion in positive ways, even if you disagree with their ideas.

A Leader Facilitates Discussion

Ask questions. Use the questions suggested in the leader/learner helps or other questions that occurred to you as you prepared for the session. Encourage others to ask questions.

Invite silent participants to contribute ideas. If someone in the group is quiet, you might say something like: "I'm interested in what you are thinking." If they seem hesitant or shy, do not pressure them to speak. Do communicate your interest.

Gently redirect discussion when someone in the group dominates. You can do this in several ways. Remind the group as a whole that everyone's ideas are important. Invite them to respect one another and to allow others the opportunity to express their ideas. You can establish a group covenant that clarifies such respect for one another. Use structured methods such as going around the circle to allow everyone a chance to speak. Only as a last resort, speak to the person who dominates conversation after the group meeting.

Be willing to say, "I don't know." A leader is also a learner. You are not "teaching" a certain content to a group of "students." Instead, you are helping others and yourself to engage the great themes of the Bible as points of crossing to contemporary life and faith formation.

Introducing the Great Theme

CREATION

LIVING IN AND AS GOD'S CREATION

The title, CREATION: LIVING IN AND AS GOD'S CREATION, poses not only the theme but the tension of this unit. Every human being lives in God's creation. That is a given, an act of God's grace; but does every human being live *as* God's creation? That is a choice, an act growing out of human faithfulness. This book will reflect upon what it means to live today in the midst of such grace and such choice. These reflections on contemporary life will be in dialogue with critical biblical texts. For the most part, the portions of Scripture to be used will be from Wisdom Literature: Psalms, Job, Ecclesiastes, and Proverbs, with a pair of Gospel texts from Mark and John included for reasons that will become apparent in those chapters.

In Judaism, wisdom is not a synonym for intellect, nor can it be reduced to the scores on an IQ test. Hebrew wisdom has much more to do with the discernment of what is right and just in life and then conducting one's life in such ways. In other words, wisdom involves a sound integration of belief, perception, and action. Knowledge and understanding are important, but wisdom awaits the implementation of those qualities in the actions of daily living.

You may see, then, why wisdom texts mesh with the theme of living in and as God's creation. To know that we live in God's creation is fine, but such awareness intends to shape us so that we may live as God's creation. How do we live as God's creation? That is the primary concern of Israel's Wisdom Literature: life lived faithfully in the presence of God. The sessions follow three "movements" that engage such wisdom.

The opening two sessions explore foundational assertions made about creation in several psalms. Wisdom takes seriously not only matters about what it means to be human but how the whole creation forms a tapestry valued by God who fashioned and sustains it. Praise generated by wonder and awe forms the fundamental expression of our recognizing God's hands and purposes in these psalms of creation. Wisdom as "knowledge" begins in our perceiving the deep knowledge of God for our lives.

Life, however, does not constantly offer us experiences that generate praise. At other times, we encounter moments and seasons that pain us, that bewilder us, and that otherwise call into question the hospitable nature of creation. The primary texts now turn to Job, the biblical document most consumed with the question of suffering and evil in the world. Job continues to sound an important note about creation, one very much at home in a day and age concerned with random acts of violence and terror, where all of creation seems to be threatened by forces seemingly out of control. Is hope still possible? Job and the Easter text of Mark 16 urge a wisdom that does not necessarily have all the answers yet proceeds with trust. Their stories reveal that such wisdom remains a choice to be made rather than a foregone conclusion.

Having faced these difficult experiences of what it means to live in creation in the face of evil and suffering and death, what then will the choice of wisdom look like? That forms the concern of the final three sessions. The focus here will fall upon attitudes toward life influenced by God's sustaining presence and Spirit, trust of God that opens our lives to God's guidance, and living with integrity as persons and communities of faithfulness. This concluding section is by no means an attempt to minimize the difficulties of life confronted in our lives and treated in the Book of Job. Wisdom that lives in trust of God is not oblivious to the suffering and sin of the world. Indeed, the practical orientation of wisdom toward our efforts to live according to God's will urges us to speak and act with passion in those very places that deny faith's word or viability. The wisdom of trusting God takes no great effort or risk where life falls in pleasant places. The wisdom of trusting God takes extraordinary witness and finds extraordinary grace where life falls in threatening places.

CREATION: LIVING IN AND AS GOD'S CREATION. Live with those words and the wisdom they would bring and evoke over these next weeks. In the readings, in your group experiences, in your times of prayer and reflection, consider the grace and the vocation joined in this unit. We best live *in* God's creation when we remember to live as God's creation. That is the wisdom to which God calls us and with which God would bless our lives and through them all creation.

Thanks be to God!

GOD CARES FOR ALL CREATION

Psalms 8; 104

This session explores human beings and the entire natural world as God's creation. It will help us see ourselves as beings who are valued by God and who live within a natural world that is also valued by God. It will provide opportunities to celebrate God as our Creator.

GATHERING

Welcome one another. Introduce yourself to the group by sharing your name and your favorite place in the world and what makes it so. Where do you see God's care evidenced there? In what ways have those places been valued and cared for (or not) by human hands? How do those gifts in nature shed light on the way God values and cares for us? Pray together the following prayer: God of all creation, be with us as we celebrate the goodness of all you have created. Help us to experience the re-creating power of your Spirit. In Christ we pray. Amen.

19

Cable Earth News

> *Which of these stories intrigues you most? Why? What does it say to you about the value of human beings and/or the natural world? What does it reveal about how such value evokes or relates to caring? How would you write the end of the story you chose?*

Anchor: Good evening. Our correspondents have been following several stories for tonight's roundup of how it goes on planet Earth. Here's a synopsis from each one's focus segment.

Miriam: I'm reporting on an effort to clean up a stream contaminated by an accidental spill. What's unusual is that the clean-up crew is a group of residents from a juvenile detention center for whom the work forms part of their own rehabilitation.

Kim: I'm here at the entrance to this region's largest national park. As you can see through the haze formed by what the rangers attribute to exhaust fumes from increasingly heavy traffic, a whole group of vehicles have the same bumper sticker: "We're Spending Our Children's Inheritance." I'll interview the group to find out who they are, what they're spending, and why.

Daniel: I'm standing with a young woman whose name is Linda. Linda struggled for years with issues of self-worth, but she recently underwent a dramatic change after reading the words of a 3,000-year-old song known as Psalm 8.

Sharon: In this church in Alberta, newly released sex offenders come for help and guidance from a group of volunteers. I'll talk to the volunteers about how and why they render care to people whom a lot of people think should just be written off.

Anchor: We look forward to all those reports on tonight's theme: "God Cares for All Creation."

Valuing Our Existence and Creation

A pundit once observed that the only two sure things in life are death and taxes. I would affirm two prior universal conditions. Every

20

one of us lives within this created world. Every one of us lives as a human being. Our choices and actions from day to day flow from how we value each of those truths about our lives and the life of all around us.

> *What questions do you carry about the meaning or value of creation as a whole? about human existence?*

Those affirmations cannot help but raise issues inherent to religion in general and Christianity in particular. Is creation hospitable for or indifferent to life? Who are we as human beings in this creation? In this session, Psalms 8 and 104 will provide assertions of God's care for all creation.

Bracketed by Praise

Besides a common emphasis on creation, Psalms 8 and 104 share one notable structure in common. The psalmist bracketed both psalms, at beginning and ending verses, with words of praise or blessing of God. These "refrains" reflect on one hand the fact that the psalms are poetic writing, where meter and repetition are frequent companions. On a deeper level, however, this bracketing by praise serves to communicate a crucial element of their theology. Namely, everything else affirmed in these psalms traces back to this fundamental statement of God's praise as Creator of all.

Psalm 104 bears a striking resemblance to an even older Egyptian hymn of praise. The assertion of cycles and ordering made in this psalm is thus not unique to Judaism; and, in fact, the body of the psalm makes remarkably few references to the name of God. The bracketing exclamations of praise to God, however, make

> *Read Psalm 8. Begin by reading in unison verse 1a, and then read each verse individually by a different reader, closing with verse 9 in unison. Repeat the same process for Psalm 104.*
> *What do these psalms affirm about what or how God cares for creation? What do these psalms associate with human meaning or purpose? How do these psalms speak to any or all of those stories in "Cable Earth News"? Where do you find them addressing those questions you identified about the value or meaning of life at the end of that section?*

> *How would life look if all were intentional about "bracketing" all choices and actions with praise to God?*

clear that the awe and wonder experienced by many persons inside and outside of Israel at nature all stems from the crafting of God. The bracketing of praise in Psalm 8 serves an even more critical purpose in this next section.

Who Do We Think We Are?

Opinions on human worth or value vary widely; and actions, as they say, speak louder than words. Abusive actions against another call into question whether the offender really values human life. Otherwise, why treat it with such disdain? Abusive or demeaning attitudes toward oneself can be equally destructive. People who have no sense of self-worth may consider themselves beyond help, beyond deserving, or beyond God.

Psalm 8 makes an extraordinary claim and bestows a weighty vocation on human identity. The claim arises out of a question raised in the song: "What are human beings that you are mindful of them?" It is an understandable question, standing under a starlit night (verse 3), marveling at the incredible display of creation's vastness. The psalmist raises the question, already aware God "is mindful" and "cares" for human beings; but the claim is even more stunning than the sky above: "You have made [us] a little less than God." If that were not enough, the psalmist asserts a vocation as old as the Creation story itself: "You have given them dominion over the works of your hands." Dominion, in Psalm 8, however, cannot be separated from the bracketing of God's praise and sovereignty. God is not an absentee landlord who cares not a whit what we do with what has been entrusted. Psalm 104 affirms God's ongoing and continuing providence of creation. The whole of our lives and creation come under the dominion of God.

> *Where have you encountered opinions and actions that put little if any value on human worth? What was your response? When have you found yourself in situation where you questioned your own value in the sight of others or God? In what ways did faith play a role in that situation and deliverance from it?*

So how do we rightly exercise dominion? One intriguing connection comes in the use of Psalm 8 in the New Testament. In all three instances where a portion of Psalm 8 is quoted (1 Corinthians 15:27; Ephesians 1:22; Hebrews 2:6-9), the writers use this psalm in reference to the person and work of Jesus. So how did Jesus exercise dominion and instruct its practice?

The episode in which James and John request places of honor brings dominion to the forefront (Mark 10:35-45). In contrast to the conventional wisdom of power politics that "those whom they recognize as their rulers *lord* it *over* them," Jesus embodied and taught another way (Mark 10:42). "Whoever wishes to become great among you must be your servant . . . for the Son of Man came not to be served but to serve" (Mark 10:43, 45). Servanthood forms the Gospel's expression of dominion. Dominion in the life of Jesus is anything but permission to do what I please. Dominion in the garden is "not my will but yours be done" (Luke 22:42). Dominion involves power exercised on behalf of others through love.

> Dominion *comes from a Latin root* (dominus) *meaning "lord." It is, clearly, a word of power and authority. Dominion has been interpreted by some as a license to do what we please in and with the world's resources. (Resource is a word that presumes it is there to be used, with little or no distinction drawn at times between used by or used up.) Dominion in the New Testament finds its clearest connection with the term* lord *(the Greek word* kurios), *one of the chief titles for Jesus Christ.*

> *How do you see Jesus' example of servanthood addressing issues of dominion? What possibilities of transforming dominion does servanthood bring to your practice of power, to your caring for others? Where does your congregation need to grow in moving from dominion as power wielded over people to dominion as power exercised to serve others?*

Manifold Values

Psalm 104 serves as a litany for the diversity of God's gifts and providential actions in creation. Unlike Psalm 8, where the identity and

23

Create a collage of creation based on Psalm 104. Cut or tear out pictures and headlined words/phrases from magazines. In the center of the collage, paste or glue pictures and words that show the diversity and interdependence of creation. On the borders, affix words and images that reflect praise of God's fashioning of and caring for creation. If you cannot find the right pictures or words in the magazines, use markers to write or draw. Display near your worship center or another place easily seen during the session.

Make a list of elements of creation that are immediate to the area in which you live. Spend time discerning their interconnections to one another. Discuss how parts of creation that we find unappealing or even repulsive form a needed balance in the larger order of things. Move this conversation to issues of community and differences among persons. Reflect on how God's blessing may be found in, and extended to, persons and groups whom we may find difficult to be with. How can the church better help us to celebrate all the gifts of God's creation and God as Creator of all things and all persons?

vocation of humankind dominates the reflections on creation, humankind in Psalm 104 is but one of a series of God's good works that form a balance to one another. Everything feels interconnected here, not standing in isolation or of value only unto themselves but in relationship to the life that depends upon it. Streams give drink. Grass grows for cattle. Trees are watered and so give shelter to birds. God may come wrapped in light, yet even darkness creates a time when God's providing for the young lions occurs. A rich and varied tapestry of life unfolds, all made in God's wisdom.

God's wisdom even undergirds the things that make us uncomfortable. The Semitic peoples developed stories that expressed their fear of the sea. It was a place of sea monsters and peril. It was a place where demons dwelled (hence the reaction of fear and "It is a ghost!" when disciples caught sight of Jesus walking on the waves). Yet in the providence of God, the sea forms a vast reservoir of living things made by God. Even the feared Leviathan is reduced (or exalted) to play. All of these things, even the ones that create fear, go valued by God.

Where and when do you find it most diffi-cult to accept yourself as cared for by God? Find a partner. Share with each other a struggle you have had or may still have in that area of your life.

At times, we resist such an inclusive vision of creation: whether of nature in general or of human beings in particular. We prefer our company to be like us, and we prefer to think God likes us best of all. Our enemies should be the enemies of God. Our fears should equate to the fears of God or, at least, the fears God will stamp out for us by removing them. Psalm 104 provides a gently liturgical affront to all such carefully constructed worlds of our own preferences and resemblances. God's dominion, which is to say God's care, is for all creation.

The works of God are far more manifold than they are uniform. The psalmist invites us to encompass all creation with the blessing of God by our very spirits.

God's Care Embracing Our Lives

We do not live in the same day and age as the psalmist, but we do live with similar issues. As with Psalm 8, we may wonder about our value. The idea of dominion might seem far removed if, and when, we struggle with issues of control over our own lives and habits—and, sometimes, addictions. Natural disasters may cause us to ask whether creation really is a hospitable place. Then again, moves into new neighbor-hoods, new jobs, or new churches may create the same tension. In a world and society that so values the idea of our being self-made women and men, how do we make sense of being creations of God, embraced with care?

Find a partner. Talk about the ease and/or difficulty of trust for you. Identify an instance where you affirm gratitude for God's providential care in and for your life. Talk about how that may encourage you to exercise such care toward others and to cre-ation as a whole.

Then as now, the psalms invite us to see our lives surrounded and embraced by the grace of God. The psalms begin and end with an act of trust in the offer of praise to the Creator for healing presence and providential care. They beckon us to make that same move of trust.

Our Care for All Creation

This session opened with an imagined news broadcast of four stories. Some of them could be true. Some of them, in fact, are true. The community in which I live houses a juvenile detention facility. Part of the youths' rehabilitation occurs not only in classrooms and counseling offices but in outdoor projects of replanting and reclamation. Seeing the world around you change can, on occasion, serve as a reminder that the world within can change. Another true story involves a group of Christians in Canada that have created a program that seeks to help released sex offenders re-enter society in a way that blends accountability with compassion.

Common to all four stories is God's handiwork of creation that bears need of care. It is not enough to say God cares for creation, so everything will be fine regardless of what we do. God fashioned us in the image of God, which means not so much that we look like God but that we have the potential of acting in ways that reveal God in and on behalf of creation. Faith that declares that God cares for all creation invites faithful action, extending that same care ourselves to the persons and world around us. Seen in the bracketing of our lives with God's praise, our own caretaking for creation does not become an imposed duty exercised out of fear for what God will do to those who do not care. Rather, our caretaking for the environment and for one another transforms into a joyous response and celebration of the God who surrounds us and all creation with grace that brings life and enables vocation. Thanks be to God!

Think of and suggest programs and projects where you and/or your congregation are involved in caring for human and natural creation. Listening to the four news stories again, identify ideas for new ministries of caring that you and your congregation might consider. Decide on two or three of these as priorities for your church. Discuss a strategy for bringing them to the attention of officers and boards responsible for such ministries of caretaking.

CLOSING WORSHIP

Reflect on what this session has triggered in your mind and spirit. Sing or read one or more verses from a hymn that celebrates God's ongoing care and providence in creation (for example, "I Sing the Almighty Power of God" or "Cantemos al Senor").

Close by offering a litany sentence prayer. Individual prayers in gratitude for or in hope of God's care in creation will each be followed by the group responding with "Bless God Our Creator."

WE PRAISE GOD WHO CREATED AND KNOWS US

Psalm 139:145

This session explores the qualities of God who created us. It will help us to identify reasons for praising God and will provide opportunities to offer prayers of praise to God

GATHERING

Welcome one another. Write on a slip of paper a specific reason you have for praising God this day. Identify in that reason why God is to be praised. (For example, if the reason is "the love of my daughter," why praise God rather than the daughter?) Read your reason aloud. Pray together the following prayer: We thank you and praise you, God, for all your gifts to us and for all the things that lead us to praise you. We thank you for this day, this time, and for your presence. Help us to know more deeply who you are and how you are revealed in creation and in our lives. In Christ we pray. Amen.

A Letter to a Newborn Child

Dearest Tracy,

We have been waiting and hoping for you for so long, and now you are here. What a wonder you are! Looking at you is to look on the miracle of life itself. You are already becoming older and taking in more of the world around you. We hope in that world within you that you know how much you are loved and how much potential you have.

At the moment, you are small enough to cradle in our arms. It will not be this way for long. You will grow. Your legs will soon take you places on your own, even as that mind of yours that is absorbing the sights and sounds and smells and tastes and touches of this world with such speed right now will also take you places on your own.

For some years to come, we will go with you to those places: sometimes instructing and guiding, sometimes close at hand or far away. Someday you will take flight on your own; but even then, we will be with you in spirit. We will still look on you with wonder, we will still see in you the miracle of life. We will still love you.

We have decided to read this letter to you every night for the first year of your life before you go to sleep. It will not be a lullaby to put you to sleep. Rather, it will be a seed we hope to plant in that expanding mind and spirit of yours. Some say you will not understand the words. We say, they will be there, deep inside you; and when that day comes when you leave home for school or a job, we will give you this letter to carry with you. So you may know who you truly are.

With deep love,
Your Parents

> *If this infant "hears" those words read to her, what qualities of character would you expect to develop in her? What difference would it make for a child to hear these affirmations from a parent? from a teacher? from a pastor? What changes, if any, would you make in the letter if the signature line was "God" instead of "your parents"?*

Would that every child born into this world knew and experienced such love from those who bore them life. Would that every parent took

> *Look through your church hymnal. Select favorite hymns of praise. Identify the qualities of God that summon praise in those songs. What do they reveal of God as Creator? of God's knowledge of us?*

the time to communicate such care and love and hope in each child brought into this world.

God does. God communicates such care and love and hope in us and in all creation. Psalm 139 praises God's wondrous fashioning and knowledge of us and the steadfast way God seeks us out with love and grace. Psalm 145 connects that praise with God's created order as a whole, at the core of which God comes revealed in grace and steadfast love and compassion "over all that he has made" (145:9). In this session, we will delve more deeply into those reasons we praise the God who created us and knows us and seeks us out with a love that will not let us go.

Songs of Praises

Psalms 139 and 145 share in common cause to praise God, though they do so from two distinct perspectives. Psalm 139 is an intensely personal reflection. The language is all "you" and "me." At stake in this psalm is the intimacy of God's knowledge of human beings coupled with the degree to which God seeks us out and remains present with us no matter where we might venture.

> *Read Psalm 139. What does this psalm assert about the qualities of God revealed in our creation? Read Psalm 145 aloud in the following sections: verses 1-2, 4-7, 8-9, 10-13, and 14-21. After each section, read aloud in unison verse 3. What does this psalm identify as reasons to praise God? Which of the two psalms appeals most to you? Why?*

Psalm 145 takes a far wider perspective. While the individual voice of the psalmist praises, the causes trace more to God's works throughout creation and across generations and for all living things. Look closely at the words: "All" occurs sixteen times in these verses. This sense of comprehensiveness is also reflected in its acrostic structure. (See "Acrostic Form in Hebrew Poetry.")

Acrostic Form in Hebrew Poetry

Acrostic *in Hebrew and other poetry describes a structure of writing that is based on the letters of the alphabet. The most typical form, as seen in the Hebrew of Psalm 145, begins each line with a successive letter of the alphabet (line 1 starts with "a," line 2 with "b," and so on). There are 22 letters in the Hebrew alphabet. Lines do not necessarily correspond to verses, so that while Psalm 145 has 21 verses, it has 22 lines each beginning with one of the letters. Some explain acrostic as a device to help in memorization. Others see it, as in Psalm 145, also adding a sense of completeness or wholeness to the topic at hand. Everything is here from A–Z!*

God Is . . . Faithful and Gracious in All

Imagine you were given the task of describing God to someone who had never heard of God and therefore had no understanding or experience. Where would you begin? How would you proceed from the statement: God is . . .? If you followed the way the Hebrew Scriptures give witness to God, you might want to change the starting point of that task from describing "who God is" to narrating "what God does." One of the fundamental truths about Judaism is that our knowledge of God comes through God's actions. Read through the entire Old Testament, and you will find few passages that deal with theology in the abstract. There is little speculation about the nature of God. There is, however, much witness about the activity of God in creation, in deliverance, and in the formation of community. Maybe you recall the line from the movie *Forrest Gump*: "Simple is as simple does"? To paraphrase that line: When it comes to the witness of God in the Hebrew Scriptures, "God is as God does."

How do you end the sentence, "God is . . ."?

What is the importance of our knowledge of God being grounded in God's actions? In what ways does that influence the reasons for and nature of our praise? How does your congregation acknowledge and praise the activity of God in the lives of individuals and in the life of creation as a whole?

Psalm 145 concludes with a litany of God's qualities that evoke praise (verses 13b-20). "The Lord" translates the Hebrew *YHWH* or *Yahweh*, the name of God given to Moses at the burning bush in Exodus 3. Listen to the verbs that tell us who God is by what God does: *upholds, raises, opens, satisfy, fulfills, hears, saves,* and *watches over.* Justice and kindness likewise are revealed in this passage as attributes of God, qualities revealed in God's keeping of covenant with us even as God seeks those same qualities in our lives. Notice, too, how all those verbs bring God into relationship with individuals and communities in ways that give life to others.

Sometimes our praise of God veers too exclusively to matters of God's majesty and awesome character, matters that make God totally other than us. While majesty and awe certainly belong to God's character, what summons this psalm's praise are the ways in which God comes to us and gives of God's own self for our sake. Our praise of God always intends to bring us into awareness of God's relationship with us and actions on behalf of us and all creation.

We Are. . . Fearfully and Wonderfully Made

"Who God is" inevitably leads to consideration of "who we are." Opinions on that second question range widely. On one end of the spectrum, some say the essential truth of human identity in the sight of God is "utterly depraved." The famous sermon by Jonathan Edwards, "Sinners in the Hands of an Angry God," using the image of humanity as tiny spiders being held over a consuming fire by a righteous God, voices that view. On the other end of the spectrum, following the lead of Psalm 8, the answer given to our identity is "crown of creation." A motto in an earlier age spoke of our "every day, in every way, getting better and better."

Psalm 139 poses another compelling assertion of our identity: We are "fearfully and wonderfully made." We are, above all else, the handiwork of God. "Fear and wonder" are usually connected in the Hebrew Scriptures with events or occasions of God's revealing in ways that exceed understanding. So it is with our creation. We are made in ways that aptly evoke the description of "mystery." Scientifically, we still wrestle to comprehend the mysteries of the human brain and the way chemistry and biology and who knows what other disciplines combine in its function. Personally, we still wrestle to comprehend our very selves. Have you ever done something you had awareness of a reason why? Do you really understand everything there is to be understood about your personality or about your motivations?

> *Read Psalm 139:13-17. Think of ideas of what you still see as mysteries in human existence. How and where do you see these mysteries resulting from God's hand in our creation? In what ways are these mysteries a reason for praise?*

To the phrase "fearfully and wonderfully made" might also be added "fearfully and wonderfully known and sought." The first half of Psalm 139 explores God's knowledge of us, even when we would seek flight or refuge from that knowledge. The psalm touches on sensitive territory here. We do not always seek God. Whether out of guilt, or anger, or self-assertion, or other reasons, at times we would like to be out of God's sight and reach. *The Hound of Heaven* is a 19th-century poem by Francis Thompson that speaks with powerful imagery of this flight we sometimes undertake and of God's equally relentless seeking of us no matter where we go.

> *How do you respond to the psalm's portrayal of God's all-encompassing knowledge? Is it reassuring, intruding, or something else? Why? What examples from contemporary culture illustrate knowledge of us? Which illustrations are uncomfortable or disturbing to us?*

Core Confessions

The reasons for our praise of God may be almost too many to number when we think long and hard about it. On the other hand, it might

34

Think about, or even take a walk through, your church's sanctuary and/or fellowship space. Where do you see, in word or symbol, the core reasons for your congregation's praise of God?

be helpful to narrow down the reasons for our praise of God to essentials. Why? Perhaps for the same reason that Jesus once narrowed down all the hosts of laws and commandments in Judaism's written and oral traditions to two fundamental matters: Love God and love neighbor as self. The reason is to keep the core clearly in mind, to keep our eyes and hearts and actions focused on that which will help all the others fall into place.

A similar movement occurs in Psalm 145. As already noted, the psalm offers a closing litany of reasons for praise of God grounded in the character and actions of God. The psalm opens with a word of praise stretching across generations, lauding God's mighty acts and awesome deeds and abundant goodness and God's righteousness and . . . and . . . and. The list could go on indefinitely; but the psalmist made an interesting turn, inserting a formula for praise from a time long before. It is the word declared by God to Israel at a covenant renewal ceremony: Yahweh, Yahweh, a God gracious and merciful, slow to anger and abounding in steadfast love (145:8).

An Ancient Psalm

The ascription at the beginning of the psalm identifies this work with David, who reigned sometime close to the end of the 11th or the early 10th century B.C. Some scholars place this, along with the other psalms in Book Five of the Psalms, in the period at the close of exile or return in the fifth century B.C. Psalm 145:8, however, comes neither from the time of exile or David. Rather, it comes from Israel's wilderness sojourn.

These are ancient words, but they still served to summarize the core of Israel's cause for praise of God: grace, mercy, slow to judgment, full of love. How do we come to know these things? We look at what God has done. The psalmist spoke out of experience—personal and communal. We know the God who created and knows us in the same way, by the stories and experiences that arise from our lives and from the lives of the communities that sustain our faith.

At the End . . . You

The author of Psalm 139 comes to the realization that the mysteries of God finally exceed our comprehension. "I come to the end —I am still with you." The bottom line of spiritual life and journey remains the same. Not every door will be opened to us; not every matter we confront in life will resolve itself and be perfectly understood. As with the psalmist, we are like Paul who, at the close of his oft-quoted thoughts on love was led to say: For now we see in a mirror, dimly, but then we will see face to face. Now I know only in part; then I will know fully, even as I have been fully known (1 Corinthians 13:12).

> *With a partner, talk about the "old words" that still serve as compass and summary for our praise and service of God. Speak of experiences—individual and communal—that underscore their continuing truth and life today. Identify ways in which, as individuals and as a congregation, we might be better at passing on those words and framing them in new ways and with fresh imagery that help another generation experience their truth and power. Share your conversation with the entire group.*

For some, that partial knowledge spurs resentment or a claim to know more than we really do or can know. For others, however, like Paul and like the psalmist, the limits of human knowledge find peace in the trust we live in the presence of God. Even when we come to the end—the end of our wits, the end of our ability to understand, and finally the end of our lives—even then, "I am still with you."

In the end, we will not be alone. In the end, we will be loved. In the end, the One who created and knows us will hold us in grace and not let us go. To know that as our end is to know we can begin (again) to live now with courage and love and trust . . . and praise!

> *What do you see waiting at "the end"? What leads you to that belief? Discuss how what we see at the limits (of our knowledge, of our capabilities, of our lives) influences how we conduct our lives now. How would you express that in a prayer of praise?*

36

CLOSING WORSHIP

Silently consider the thoughts about God, creation, and self evoked during the session. Sing "For the Beauty of the Earth." Form a circle and join hands. Invite individuals to offer in silence or in word a prayer of praise to God. Start it off, and go clockwise around the circle. If an individual wishes to offer the praise silently, ask them to indicate when they are finished by squeezing the hand of the person on their left. Close the session by offering the following benediction adapted from Psalm 145:

God is gracious and merciful.

God is slow to anger and abounding in steadfast love.

God is good to all.

God's compassion is over all that God has made

GOD CARES WHEN ALL SEEMS HOPELESS

Job 1–3; 32:1-8; 34:10-15; 37:14-24

This session explores tragic circumstances that challenge our sense of a caring God. It will help us identify ways to experience God's presence, power, and love when life seems to be without hope.

GATHERING

Welcome one another by name. Think of ideas about places and situations that seem hopeless in the world and in your particular community. What makes them so? Silently reflect on times when you considered yourself in a hopeless situation. What were your feelings in that experience? Where did you sense God in those times, if at all? Pray the following prayer: God, help us when our faith does not serve as an escape hatch from experiences that challenge our ability to hope in your presence or care. Please hear us, and others, when we cry out from such places. Be with us as we explore the troubling story of Job in this session. In Christ we pray. Amen.

What Would You Say?

Three days ago, Trish's teenage son died in a car wreck. Alex was a senior in high school, months away from graduation and then university. Some speculated Alex might have been speeding; others said the rain, after weeks of dry weather, accounted for slick conditions on the curve. All of that seemed distant, foreign, to Trish. Reality for her focused on that coffin in the visitation room of the mortuary.

Visitors came by to pay respects. Almost everyone greeted Trish— some in silence, some seeking to put into words what was for Trish unspeakable. Some of the words of condolence that Trish heard that day include the following:

> *Place yourself in Trish's position. How does the "explanation" given by each of these expressions speak to your grief? What do these words reveal of God? Why? Think now of your own experience. What words have you spoken to others who faced such tragedy? What might you say to them now?*

- "I know exactly how you feel. My great-uncle died last year. He was a great guy, just like your son, though it'd been years since I saw him."
- "I'm so sorry for your loss. It's hard to believe the way kids take these chances."
- "It's just terrible. Terrible. But at least, you'll always have your memories."
- "God needed another beautiful flower in heaven's garden."
- "It may be hard to accept now, but you have to know it was God's will."

Suffering Is Real

To live in creation is to be acquainted firsthand with suffering and tragedy, including situations that defy rationalization or explanation. Some individuals find it hard to see their way forward through such times. Life is frozen in grief. Death seems almost preferable to life. Other individuals move ahead by denying the ambiguities of innocent suffering. They employ a rigid moral "cause and effect" understanding, so that everything becomes a matter of guilt ("you get what you deserve in life") or God's will ("absolutely everything that happens is

40

the result of God's will for our lives"). Still others face the abyss of suffering and tragedy, their own and others, with a stoic silence. Society and even the church have sometimes abetted that attitude. When grief brings deep feel-

> *What methods of dealing with grief have you encountered in society and in church?*

ings of anger to the surface or takes the form of bitter complaint, the encouragement is to silence and to "keep it under control." We sedate people through grief, philosophically or medicinally; but grief submerged is only grief delayed.

There Once Was a Man Named Job

The Book of Job presents a powerful expression of faith voiced in lament. Job will not give up his own life (1:9-10). Job will not accept the accusation of his guilt as cause nor will he accept what has happened as an act of God's justice. Job will not be silent.

The church does not always know what to do with Job. He speaks with such power and passion not only to his "friends" but to God, it might seem he verges over the edge of respectfulness. However, remember that what Job does is refuse to let go of God. His lament trusts that God will hear. Job reminds us that lament can be a powerful and needed expression of faith when we enter times and situations that make no sense and bring untold suffering. Through this book, we learn about a faith that is honest to God in the moments when we feel that God is most distant—when all seems hopeless.

What do we know about Job—the book or the character? The name Job does not occur elsewhere in Israel's history or stories, although parallel names are found in other Near Eastern writings. Likewise, his territory of Uz is equally unclear, with some associations to the regions of either Edom or Aramea.[1] We do not know when the Book of Job was written. There is no identification of contemporary events or historical figures that would suggest a date. Speculation runs

> *What prior understandings of Job (the character and/or the book) do you bring to this session? What experiences of suffering do you bring to this session?*

41

from the tenth century B.C. through the fourth century B.C.[2] The inter-pretation of Job as a book written to address the crisis and experience of exile and all of its attendant questions about God's role in that national tragedy has a strong following but is not conclusive.[3]

Babylonian Theodicy

Did Job's author have in mind other literature or stories that explore suffering and God's role? A text known as the "Babylonian Theodicy" (theodicy refers to the problem of God and the origin of evil) survives from perhaps the 11th or 10th century B.C. from Mesopotamia. It consists of a dialogue between one who has endured great suffering and a friend. While this structure resembles Job, the outcomes differ greatly. In this other text, the one who suffers and the friend eventually settle on a measure of blame on the "gods"; and there is no concluding speech or response from those gods.[4]

The clearest element of Job is its structure: two shorter prose sections (Chapters 1–2 and 42:7-17) enclose a much larger poetic section (3:1–42:6). The opening prose section relates the story of why what happens to Job happens and, in the process, raises disturbing stories about God's hand in this as well as the nature and identity of a character who is referred to as 'ha-satan' in Hebrew. This is not a proper name as is translated in many translations of the Bible. The words mean *Satan*, can mean "the accuser" or "the adversary." The closing prose section speaks of the restoration to Job of what he had lost. Other hard questions complicate its seeming resolution. For example, how do you restore dead children with new ones? Does the grief and emptiness not remain?

Read Job 1–2. If you could stop the text at two points and ask questions of what you had just read, where would you stop? What would you ask? Why? What is the image of God you find in these chapters? What is the image of human existence? How do those viewpoints compare and contrast with your own?

In between the prose comes the powerful poetry that contains the dialogue (speeches alternating between Job and the friends) and then the voice of God from the whirlwind. It is in the poetry that the controversy and lament, blame and appeals for justice, find eloquent voice. It is in the voice from the whirlwind that we hear the enigmatic response of God, whose answer to Job is no answer at all but an unceasing set of questions.

Lament and Faithfulness

Reading the Book of Job is not for the faint of heart or the tame of spirit. Faced with an unimaginable progression of suffering and then unrelenting waves of blame cast his way, Job does not go quietly and timidly into the night. "Let the day perish in which I was born," he begins (3:1); and he does not relent. He goes on time and again to bring to the surface his pain and grief. He insists on a hearing by God that he may be found just and innocent; and that is the opening verdict rendered by the narrator and God: "blameless and upright" (1:1). The Book of Job is a lament, a cry to God to be heard.

The church often finds lamenting a difficult element of our tradition to affirm. Many of the psalms are laments; but by and large we prefer psalms of praise and thanksgiving to those of "How long O Lord" and "Why have you forsaken me/us?" Lamenting bares our spirits before God. Perhaps we shy away from that as individuals and as communities because it also moves us to bare our spirits before ourselves. We may not like to admit the anger or questions or denial we sometimes carry with

Read Job 3:1-9 and 14:1-6. Designate one end of the room as "absolutely yes," the other end as "absolutely no," the middle as "I don't know," and the remaining space as varying degrees of agreement or disagreement. Ask the following questions, and then stand in the room according to your response. After each time of standing, discuss why you stand where you do, for example, (1) I would speak and believe as Job if I experienced what he did; (2) I have spoken and believed as Job at some point in my life; or (3) I don't think people should talk to God like Job does.

When and why have you engaged in lament? Does your congregation allow and encourage individuals and the community to lament? If not, why? How does lamenting connect with the narratives of Palm/Passion Sunday?

us. Yet, lamenting serves a powerful role in spiritual life and formation. It opens the whole of our lives to God; and in doing so, it opens the whole of our lives to God's healing and hope. It does not hide dark corners and unresolved questions. It brings them to light, raises them in prayer and confession, and waits on God's grace. Lamenting is an expression of faith because it keeps the dialogue with God open and honest and true to life.

With Friends Like These

Job's friends start off on the right track. They hear of his suffering. They leave their homes and their agendas and come to comfort and console Job. They sit with him for seven days and seven nights—in silence.

Maybe they should have left it that way. Once the friends start to talk, compassion soon yields to finger pointing:

Eliphaz: "Think now, who that was innocent ever perished?" (4:7). *Well, let's see. How about Kosovo or Darfur or maybe the ovens of Auschwitz?*

Bildad: "If your children sinned against [God], he delivered them into the power of their transgression" (8:4). *That would be a nice balance, the children dying because they deserved it. Unfortunately, it has nothing to do with the explanation in the prose story. It still has nothing to do with children who get hit by drunk drivers or shot by random drive-bys who miss their targets and hit the bystanders.*

Zophar: "Know then that God exacts of you less than your guilt deserves" (11:6). *Time out! This story does not begin with Job's guilt but with his innocence. Zophar claims to know the mind of God and, in the process, gets things backwards: a not uncommon claim and not*

44

uncommon result for his modern-day descendants.

Elihu presents the most interesting case of the friends. Many scholars believe the poetic section originally ended with 31:40b ("The words of Job are ended). In that theory, Elihu represents a later addition to the book, a case strengthened (but not proven conclusively) because of language issues and quotes from Job's earlier speeches and strong allusions, if not quotes, of the not-as-yet given speech of God from the whirlwind.[5] In many ways, Elihu more than the other friends possesses the "right answers." Yet words alone will not suffice to respond to Job's lament. Elihu, in that his words remain like the others an invitation to argument rather than encounter, does not go far enough.

> *Think of an experience where you have had friends seek to console or comfort you in some difficult situation that they did not totally understand. What did you find most helpful in their words? their actions? What did you find least helpful? How has that influenced you in the way you approach others in such situations?*

Finding and Giving Hope

The Book of Job, and life, presents us with a fundamental challenge. Tragedy happens. Unfairness and injustice strike down the innocent. Job is not all that unique. The effect of the book is to focus on particular experiences that are common to living in this created order.

The challenge is in answering the question, What do we then do? The religious aspect of that question is, How then do we live with God? We have noted already, directly or indirectly, some of the possible options. We can ignore this creation and God. We can determine to live by the code of what-

> *Read Job 32:1-8. Discuss Elihu's initial reluctance to speak in light of your experiences of community and tradition. How does his anger surface in contemporary settings where old solutions or ideas do not seem to be working? Read Job 34:10-15. In what ways might these words bring hope to hopeless situations? What more, if anything, might be needed for them to accomplish that purpose for Job? for us?*

Create a maze of chairs and tables in the meeting space. Turn off the lights as much as is (safely) possible. Form pairs, and have one member lead his or her partner through the maze. Change places so that the leaders are now the followers. During the maze time, read aloud Job 37:14-23 during both walks through the maze.

After the experience, reflect on the walk and the words. What made it possible to trust? What insights might that experience bring concerning how God can be trusted to lead us when we do not clearly see the way?

ever makes us feel good at the present moment because there may be no next moment. Materialism and consumerism act out this option. In the most extreme form of this, we might choose to end our lives (suicide) or end any thought of God (deicide). We can rationalize the experience of suffering and evil and leap to the assertion it falls only upon those who deserve it (according to the friends of Job). We can deny the existence of suffering and evil, that it is only an "appearance." In other words, since we are spiritual beings, the things that happen to this body or this earth do not really matter; or, as in the case of Job, we can live with a faith that, on one hand, cries out against the suffering and injustice, and on the other hand holds on to God in hope.

Job is not an exercise in academic theorizing. Job is an invitation to understand how and where to find hope and how to give hope. Job is an invitation to search in deep and dark places for that which brings light. The hope implicit in this book is not about escaping the world nor even controlling it but living in this world and refusing to let go of God. Holding on and walking, even in darkness and in tragedy, is trusting in God's leading.

46

CLOSING WORSHIP

Form a circle, and join hands. Think back to the story of Trish that was part of this session's opening. What would your hopes be for her in light of the conversations and activities in this session? Identify individuals or groups in your community and beyond who struggle with suffering and tragedy and wonder about God's role or place in it. After each name or group, offer this prayer in unison: God, out of suffering and lament, bring hope and new life.

Hold these persons in prayer through this week, and consider any action you might take that would be an expression of friendship and faith and that would offer God's love to unanswered questions and unresolved experience.

[1]From The New Interpreter's Bible, Vol. IV (Abingdon Press, 1995); page 328.
[2]From The New Interpreter's Bible; page 325.
[3]From The New Oxford Annotated Bible (Oxford University Press, 2001); page 625; and Eerdmans Dictionary of the Bible (William B. Eerdmans, 2000); page 716.
[4]From The New Interpreter's Bible; pages 329-33.
[5]From The New Interpreter's Bible; pages 321-22.

Session

4

GOD OFFERS LIFE AND HOPE

Job 38:1-4, 16-17; 42:1-6; Mark 16

This session explores the power and hope of life over death through the resurrection of Jesus Christ. It will help us to claim this hope for ourselves in daily life and in life beyond death.

GATHERING

Greet one another. Think of questions about life and death for which you have no clear answers. Write those questions on one or more large sheets of paper. Discuss how those questions affect your ability to hope and to live a hopeful life. What sort of perspective and trust enables us to live with the questions? Pray the following prayer: God, we know that there is much to life that we do not know. Lead us and empower us to live with hope in the midst of life and in the awareness of death. In Christ we pray. Amen.

Power and Hope in the Face of Death

Try to imagine yourself in Sempangi's shoes. What would enable you to speak as he spoke and to pray for those he prayed for? How does this episode and the comments following speak of the hope and faith you hold?

Companions in Christ: Way of Grace shares the following illustration of hope in the face of death: "Kefa Sempangi, a pastor in Uganda during Idi Amin's reign of terror, lived to tell the following story: He had just celebrated the Easter service when a death squad entered the vestry. The men told him they were there to kill him. Asked if he had any final words to say, Sempangi replied, 'I am a dead man already. My life is dead and hidden in Christ. It is your lives that are in danger, you are dead in your sins. . . . I will pray for you.'

"Fear relies on the threat of death, a threat made all the more powerful when we have not faced the truth of our own mortality. But when death is prepared for, when God is trusted beyond death's horizon, fear dissipates. Life can then be lived to its fullest and freest in every moment."[1]

Few of us face situations as horrific as this. However, every one of us will at one time or another face the reality of death. Is there something or some One whose power and authority may give us confidence and hope in that moment? In this session, passages from Job and Mark's Easter story provide the settings to what it means to have hope in life, even and especially at the horizon line where physical life ends.

Encountering God

Write the following on a sheet of paper: "Hope is . . ." How would you finish that sentence to define and/or illustrate hope's meaning? What empowers us to have such hope? Discuss your responses with others in the group.

It has been a long time since God as a character played an active role in the drama of Job; but after the friends have spoken, after Job has raised his lament and sought justice, God speaks from a whirlwind. In the Old Testament, the word *whirlwind* is frequently associated

Imagine yourself in the place of Job. Skim the questions asked in Chapters 38–41. How do these questions, individually and collectively, shape your sense of a caring God, your hope, or what it means to live as a human being in this creation?

with moments of encounter with God, as when Elijah is taken up to heaven in a whirlwind (2 Kings 2:1).

What God speaks are not answers to questions of where God has been in Job's suffering or larger issues of where and how evil and innocent suffering comes into this world. Instead, God asks nearly four chapters of questions that neither Job nor any other human being is capable of answering. The questions consistently draw on aspects of nature and creation, real and legendary.

To this point, Job has been living with unresolved question. Now, the answer from God brings not answers but only more questions.

Something hidden to those of us who do not read Hebrew also occurs in these chapters, and it is of enormous consequence. When Job 38:1 announces that the Lord answers Job, the Hebrew word there is *Yahweh* or *YHWH*. This is the name of God that occurs in Exodus 3 when Moses encounters God at the burning bush, the name by which the God who delivered Israel from Egypt would be known. It is a peculiar name; its meaning derives somehow from the Hebrew verb "to be" and can be translated: "I am who I am" or "I cause to be what I cause to be." This name of God has not been used since the prose of Chapter 2. It is as if Job and his friends have been engaged in a religious conversation about God in general rather than the Holy One on whom the story turns. Now, Yahweh comes to center stage at the book's close. Yahweh will speak for God's self. God will be encountered.

What do you experience as the difference between conversation about God and encounter with God? How does this long series of questions speak to you about that difference not only in Job but in your life?

"I had heard of you by the hearing of the ear, / but now my eye sees you" (Job 42:5-6). Hope, for Job, had initially been in pleas for vindication, in cries that his case be heard by God so that God might assert Job's innocence in the face of his accusers. Now, it would seem, hope takes a much different orientation. Job's tragic circumstances remain. Although the prose conclusion offers an account of restoration to even greater wealth than before, there remains the nagging question and grief over the dead children. Yet Job makes this confession of encounter with God *before* any acts of restoration. They are almost irrelevant to the movement and power of this story. Even in the face and experience of tragedy and death, God sojourns with us in our questions. God does not bring all their answers (at least,

> *Read Job 42:1-5. When and where have you moved from "hearing about" to "seeing" God? In what ways would you consider or speak of that as an encounter with God? How? Why? What difference has that experience made in your ability to hope?*

not now), but encounter and covenant with God as our companion and hope remain intact. That is what, or who, Job sees at the end. Hope remains, for God remains.

Holy Fear

Some parts of the biblical witness leave us scratching our heads, not unlike Job in the face of this cascade of rhetorical questions. Among the experiences that generate such questions is fear. Sometimes it is fear of the unknown as when Moses "hid his face" before a burning bush because "he was afraid to look at God" (Exodus 3:6). Sometimes it is fear of the all too known, as when Israel fears the onslaught of a real and visible Assyrian army (2 Kings 17:1-6). There is also the fear of death, which combines the element of the unknown (what happens afterwards?) with the all too familiar experience of a loved one who no longer breathes. Death is one of those matters on which God questions Job, a question for which Job has no good answer.

> *Read Job 41:17. Recall the death of someone close to you or perhaps a death you attended or witnessed. How does that experience interact with your hope? In what ways was (or is) fear a part of your experience?*

Fear of another sort arises in Mark 16. The women go to the tomb of Jesus, planning to complete the

Read Mark 16:1-8. Create a role play where the women who went to the tomb are being interviewed at a press conference. Choose volunteers to play the roles of the women. Ask the women about their experience that morning. Ask: What did you see and hear? What did you think and feel? What made you afraid?

After the press conference, discuss as a group how the experience of Job and the experience of these women compare. What does each know of fear? What does each experience of God in the midst of those fears? How do their fears and their hopes speak to us?

preparation of his body that had been interrupted by the onset of the sabbath on Friday evening. They do not seem to have fear in the journey. The women had witnessed crucifixion, so they go expecting death. They do not even seem alarmed when they see the stone rolled away from the tomb. It had posed a potential problem as the women considered how they might get past it. The stone's unexplained removal does not alarm them. What causes fear is the unknown, the sight of a young man sitting, looking very much alive, where they anticipated finding a corpse. The women are afraid. Like Mary at the news of Gabriel (Luke 1:29-30), like shepherds on the Bethlehem hillside (Luke 2:10), like disciples on a storm-ravaged but Jesus-calmed sea (Matthew 8:23-27), they fear. The women fear the unexpected. You might call theirs, like that of those others before them, "holy" fear. For it is a fear borne of what God can do that surpasses our expectations. Even when the women are assured they need not be afraid, fear continues. "Terror and amazement" seize them. Fear can control our lives when we do not yet realize or trust in whose hands life and future rests, in whom we may hope.

Where Do We Find Hope?

The young man at the tomb informs the women to tell Peter and the others that Jesus goes ahead of them to Galilee where he may be seen by them. You would think the gospel would head the disciples, soon to be apostles, straight back to Jerusalem to confront and confound those who crucified Jesus with the news they had it all wrong. However, the direction is to Galilee. That is where hope is to be found. Why? Perhaps because that is where it all started. Most of the disciples were Galileans. Galilee was home. Galilee was family. Galilee was business as usual. Hope, the message of life, the bewildering and hardly-to-be-believed news of resurrection has to go back to Galilee.

> *What do you find most difficult about living the faith in the place where you live? How and from whom do you encounter Jesus in the ordinary places and persons of your life? Where do you find hope, and how do you live with hope where you live?*

The word *hope* is encouraging to most of us. To be sure, some want to find faith, courage, and hope in the exotic locales and spectacular choices that come only once in a lifetime. However, most of us need to find hope in all the usual places of our living. Among family and friends we know and who know us warts and all, in our vocations, in our relationships, in our temptations to cut corners, and in all such places, we need to find hope. Jesus called those disciples in such places back in Galilee; and in order to find him again, in order to follow him again, the ones who fled into the darkness would need to go to Galilee.

Not many of us are called by Jesus to live in foreign places. Most of us find the gospel's testing not in the face of what is alien but in the plain sight of what is familiar. We, too, will meet Jesus, if we meet him at all, in our own Galilee.

Hope as Our Unfinished Story

A number of ancient Greek manuscripts of Mark end with 16:8. One manuscript concludes with an expanded version of verse 8 that relates the women telling Peter and the others about what they saw and then a word about Jesus sending out the proclamation of salvation from them (it is sometimes called "the shorter ending"). Other manuscripts conclude with the so-called "longer ending" of Mark, which consists of verses 9-20. Neither of those alternate endings is considered original to Mark. Some scholars suggest there was a longer ending to Mark that had been lost, and these were substitutes. Many believe, however, the Gospel originally did end with verse 8.

As a group, write an end to Mark's Gospel. Write it based on what you do as individuals and as a community of faith to embody your hope and to witness to life in the face of death. Do not be afraid to note places where the ending is still unclear or where you and others still struggle with how to put such faith into practice. For identifying those places may well reveal to you and your church where you still need to grow from "hearing" about God to "seeing" God in your actions and witness.

An unusual thing occurs in this "first" ending of Mark. It concludes with an incomplete sentence. The translation of the Greek would more literally be "They were afraid, for . . . " For what? for whom? On the surface, this might seem an unsatisfactory way to conclude. There should be more certainty. There should be more of a sense of mission. There should be less fear and more hope. There should be a proclamation, not "they said nothing to anyone." The Gospel should not be an unfinished story!

Or should it? As the Gospel ends now, the decision about faith and hope is left squarely with the listener. The news of Easter becomes not what three women may have seen and heard and did about it 2,000 years ago but what you and I see and hear and do about it now. In one sense, the Gospel's ending makes our closing passage from Job all the more pertinent as to how we claim this hope as our own. "I had heard of you by the hearing of the ear, / but now my eye sees you" (Job 42:5-6). For Job, profound as his faith and insistence upon holding on to God had been to this point, something happens in that process of facing questions that could not be answered. Job encounters God; and in that encounter, faith transforms from the realm of ideas to the realm of experience. No one else—not his friends, not Elihu—could do that for

Write about your thoughts on times when faith has moved from ideas or propositions into experience. What triggered that transition? In what ways has that experience formed the hopes you carry and the way you live? how you face the limits of mortality? As you are willing, share those thoughts with others in the whole group or in small groups. Discuss how hope empowers life, even in the face of death.

him. It remained for Job to determine the One to be trusted, even and especially when ideas and rationalizations reached their eventual end.

The Easter narrative presents an extraordinary message. It says that the most fundamental horizon line, our mortality as human beings, faces a power greater even than it. It is not an affirmation that can be proven. It is not an affirmation that relies on "answers" or knowledge, as Job's friends sought to relegate relationship with God. Job faced questions that led him to understand there is a Power in this universe grander than any understanding that might be grasped by the human mind. The women at the tomb faced an open question that there is a Power in this universe that does not answer to death. Mark leaves that narrative hanging in mid-sentence, perhaps intentionally, as a witness to our authoring the end for ourselves. Does the Gospel need to end in fear, or can our lives write it to end in trust and hope? Pastor Sempangi answers the latter to be true.

CLOSING WORSHIP

Reread the story and words of Pastor Sempangi. Identify situations and persons where you see hope and faithfulness embodied in the midst of life and the face of death. As you name each of those places or persons, say together the words of Job: "I had heard of you by the hearing of the ear, / but now my eyes see you." Close with the following prayer: O God, thank you for bringing life in Jesus Christ, in whose name we pray. Amen.

[1]From *Companions in Christ: Way of Grace*, by John Indermark (Upper Room Books, 2004); page 89.

Session

5

GOD OFFERS MEANING
AND PEACE IN JESUS CHRIST

Ecclesiastes 1:1-11; 3:1-21; John 20:19-23

This session will explore questions about the purpose and meaning of our lives. It will help us consider God's timing as we set priorities in our daily lives.

GATHERING

Welcome one another to the gathering. Post a banner that says, "Do you know what time it is?" Identify different ways in which that question can be understood and/or answered. Reflect on how considering the right (or wrong) time has influenced a decision you have made about a relationship, a career issue, or anything else. In what ways does the perception of time in our lives influence our search for meaning or our experience of peace? What have such things to do with faith? Pray the following prayer: God of all time, open us to the times you give to us and to the meaning and peace we may find in all these times. In Christ we pray. Amen.

Can You Help Us?

James: Thanks for meeting with us, Pastor Connie. We've got a tough decision to make.

Susan: We remember when you talked about how hard it was for you to leave your former parish to come here but how it seems to have gone so well for you here.

Pastor Connie: It was, and it has. So, what are you facing?

James: I've got a job offer, a big step up in responsibility and pay. Plus it's on the coast, and we've always wanted to live by the ocean.

Susan: I could probably find a good teaching position there, and we could afford a larger house.

Pastor Connie: Sounds great, (*pause*) but I'm not hearing your usual enthusiasm about things.

James: I'd be on the road way more than I am now. Right now, I can pretty much go to all of the kids' activities. After the change, I'd be lucky to have one evening a week with Susan.

Pastor Connie: Let me ask you something. What do you think about the timing of this?

James: We kind of hoped you'd say whether it's the right time (*nervous laughter*).

Susan: Not that you'd tell us what to do, but you and Frank had to decide when you came here about the time being right. How did you know?

Pastor Connie: *Know* is probably not quite the right word for our decision. *Trust* or *hope* maybe. We had a sense of it being fitting; and, no, I won't tell you what to do (*laughter*). But listen to yourselves and

> *Would trust in what is right or trust in God help you? With whom do you identify in that story: the couple, the pastor, or the children? Why? What experiences lead you in those directions? What is your sense of the interplay of timing, trust, and meaning in this situation and in situations you have faced?*

your feelings. Think about what you both most want out of life for yourselves and for your children. Don't be afraid to look at how God might be at work here.

James: But was it clear to you, the timing and all?

Pastor Connie: When we made the decision, we felt at peace. We felt that peace three years before when I turned down a call to another congregation and stayed there. Some things just have their time. Trust your sense of what's right for one another and your children. Trust God. Does that help?

The search for understanding the rightness of time for this or that decision is a universal one in human life. Sometimes the search is weighed down with stress and anxiety over the abundance of things we have or over the things we do not have. At other times, however, we burden the decisions we make with second thoughts, regrets, and an unceasing litany of "what ifs." However, there are moments of grace when we emerge from the quest for the rightness of time with choices that bring a strong sense of peace.

Christian faith trusts that there is a purposefulness to our lives and opportune seasons. Part of how we find the gift of peace in our lives comes in trusting those purposes and discerning the opportunities God places before us to act in timely ways.

> *Where and how do you experience peace? Imagine you were told to say in one sentence what gives your life meaning. What would you say? What are your experiences and decisions that would back up what you say?*

Our two passages from Ecclesiastes can be helpful in framing the discussion of such opportune times; but they only go so far, for deeply imbedded in their messages is a certain world-weariness and resignation to time. To balance those texts is the Gospel passage from John. In John's perspective, life is not an endless cycle where nothing new ever occurs. A risen Jesus—a new experience in creation—bestows the Holy Spirit, God's power of renewing creation. We can be made new. We can find peace as we live in this created order as God's new creation in Jesus Christ.

Is It Worth It?

Read Ecclesiastes 1:1-8 and 3:19-22. How would you characterize the person who writes theses words? Do you agree or disagree with the perspectives in these passages? Why? What would you say from these verses is Solomon's wisdom?

I am told the dream is not too unusual. You are being pursued. You think you are running as fast as you can, but something is wrong. You are making no headway. Worse yet, as you look around, things are not moving by as fast as they should be. No matter how much more you extend and quicken your stride, things seem to be in slow motion. You make no progress. Sometimes, life takes on that dream-like quality of making no headway. As hard as you work at your job or in your hopes for a transformed society, nothing much changes. You begin to understand where those proverbs such as "you can't fight city hall" come from. It seems as though life is just an endless cycle of the same old thing and our efforts are vain.

Tradition attributes Ecclesiastes to King Solomon, who ruled Israel at the height of her economic and political power. While Solomon's authorship of this entire collection may or may not be historically true, it brings interesting insights into the text. What would lead one who held such

How do you respond to the Epicurean idea to eat, drink, and be merry because we may die soon? The Teacher of Ecclesiastes answers the question of life's worth, beyond the enjoyment of food and drink and work, in a singular phrase: "All is vanity" (1:1). Vanity in Hebrew does not mean what we often associate with it today— namely, a false pride. Rather, hebel has to do with something without substance or a lie. Vanity is not about standing in front of a mirror and preening. Vanity is the emptiness of something that is not what it appears. To deem life vain is to deem it empty, unreal, an illusion.[1]

> *What has ever caused you to wonder or think that all is vanity? Where and how do you see the effects of life viewed as vanity today: in personal and societal ethics; in church life; in the treatment of the environment?*

power to say such things? Solomon, you may remember, was associated with being Israel's wisest king (1 Kings 3:5-12). Some would argue that the author of Ecclesiastes (whoever it may be) writes from a philosophical stance that questions the lasting value of any action apart from what it is that brings happiness and enjoyment as in this verse: "I know there is nothing better for them than to be happy and enjoy themselves as long as they live" (3:14). Strong connections exist between the view promoted in Ecclesiastes and that of the later Greek Epicureans, made famous for their advice to eat, drink, and be merry because we may die soon.

The attitude of Ecclesiastes and the Epicureans has more than a few adherents in our day. The appeal is clear: If the world truly never does change, and if all that we do, in the end, has no lasting value—why struggle? Why not just do those things that meet one's own needs and desires—or, if we are feeling generous, those of our family and close friends—and call it good? It is a philosophy most appealing to people who live in prosperity and would just as soon keep things that way. It is a philosophy that leaves community largely defined by self-interest. It is a philosophy that sees God largely indifferent to creation outside of its making and "ordaining" (3:14).

> *Do a continuum exercise. Stand in your meeting room depending on how you view history. Designate one end of the room as all cyclical (things keep repeating). Designate the other end of the room as all linear (nothing repeats; it is all new). Designate the space in between as varying opinions one way or the other. When everyone has taken his or her place, discuss why you stand where you do. What evidence can you give to support your position?*

Is There Anything New Under the Sun?

Is life cyclical or linear? That is, do the same things just keep happening over and over again, albeit in slightly different forms and settings; or are there developments absolutely new in the cosmos and in human history?

Judaism had a variety of responses to this cyclical versus linear idea of history. Ecclesiastes falls strongly on the side of life and creation constantly and eternally moving through the same motions. So, on the one hand, the search for meaning and peace involve becoming comfortable in the cycles that come and go and accepting what is. On the other hand, the prophets tend to assert God's new actions in history that bring about change never before seen. Isaiah reminds us, "Do not remember the former things, / or consider the things of old (Isaiah 43:18). The prophet also says, "For I am about to create new heavens and a new earth" (Isaiah 65:17). In their perspective, the search for meaning and peace came through readying one's life for the transforming changes God would bring.

What about Christianity? The story of Jesus' birth and ministry and death and resurrection draws deeply on the in-breaking of the new among us. *Incarnation* is the preaching of God's sovereign realm. The meaning of *Immanuel*, "God with us," hung on a cross. Above all else there is the Resurrection. At every turn, the story of Jesus turns on the new thing God is about in Christ; and, as a result, to find meaning and peace as followers of Jesus invites us to consider the new things God would do in our lives and in our day.

Read Ecclesiastes 1:9-10 and John 20:19-20. Compare and contrast what is being said and reported in these passages. Which do you find more convincing? Why? How does each passage speak of how or where God might be encountered in life? How do those perspectives relate to your encounter of God?

Is there anything new under the sun? Much in our world argues that, no, there is nothing new under the sun. Generations have seen conflict and hatred in the Middle East erupt in acts of violence. It is as if it cannot be otherwise. The disparity between rich and poor grows and breeds contempt on both sides as it seems to have always done. The best and brightest still too often die young. Indeed, no one escapes death. It is final, but is it the end of all? Hints and glimpses of newness do peek through. Individuals and groups act with courage, even at great cost, as if some new way of peace and justice is possible;

What new thing have you seen that stirs hope in you? How does the risen Jesus factor in to your beliefs and actions on behalf of the future?

and Jesus enters the depth of human existence, even death. The women at the empty tomb hear the claim, "He is not here; for he has been raised" (Matthew 28:6), an entirely unprecedented claim that there is not only something new under the sun but that the One who is new promises to make us all new. Do you believe that?

Spirit and Peace

A curious thing happens in the Gospel of John. The gift of God's Spirit does not wait for the day of Pentecost, which occurs after Jesus' ascension (as in Luke and Acts). Rather, Jesus bestows the Holy Spirit upon the disciples on the evening of Easter. The language of "breathing" on the disciples and the Spirit's gift has deep meanings in Scripture and language. It recalls the Genesis 2 story of human creation. God formed man (*adam*) from the dust of the ground (*adamah*) and "breathed into his nostrils the breath of life" (Genesis 2:7). John 20, in a sense, portrays a new creation story as God in Christ breathes Spirit into the disciples to bring new life. The meaning even goes deeper, however, In Hebrew and in Greek, the word for "breath" and the word for "spirit" are one and the same. *Pneuma* can mean either "breath" or "spirit" (and "wind"). Jesus breathes Spirit; Jesus inspires breath. However, we would translate that the clear image is of God bestowing new life into the disciples and through them (and us) into all of creation.

Read John 20:21-22. Talk about ways in which the gift of Spirit is experienced as breath by you and by your church community. Look through your church's hymnal at songs having to do with God's Spirit. Identify the imagery there that is associated with breath and breathing. Compose a prayer that speaks of the Spirit's work and gift in terms of breath and breathe. Share your prayers with one another. Identify ways to share them with the congregation.

Twice in John 20:19-22 the greeting Christ brings is

"peace." In the first instance (verse 19), it implicitly serves as a counter to the fear identified. A number of times in Scripture, the word spoken to humans bewildered by encounter with God is "Do not fear" (Mary, the shepherds, the disciples on the stormy sea, for example). Here, however, "peace be with you" serves as the gift that disarms fear. The second use of the greeting "peace" occurs immediately before Jesus commissions the disciples and bestows the Spirit. Jesus had earlier spoken of peace in John 14:27, in the face of his imminent departure from them in death. Changing times and circumstances may come, but the gift of God's peace to calm fears and empower service remain.

There are times when answers about life's meaning may seem difficult. Tragedy still happens to the faithful. Injustice still claims the innocent. The question, "What does it mean?" will not always find ready or easy answers. However, in those times especially, "peace be with you" offers a blessing and a promise that cannot be measured in its value. A life without peace is a life of anxiety and fretting. Without peace, it does not matter how much wealth you can claim on a 1040 tax form or how much personal or national security you can enforce. Peace runs deep. It is a matter of Spirit. It is the assurance that our lives are valued by and held in the grace of God, no matter what.

> *Where and when do you experience peace in your life? How do you see the gift of peace and the gift of Spirit connected? What do they have to do with the meaning you find in and for your life?*

Seasons in Our Lives

The writer of Ecclesiastes beautifully portrays the variety of times in which we live. Even there, we may wonder about some of the affirmations: When is it right to hate? (3:8). On the whole, the words capture a deep truth about human life, the importance of timeliness and timing.

In the Judeo-Christian heritage, we cannot fully consider such issues of seasonableness without seeking to discern, as we are able, God's timing in things. We need to take care not to attribute all things that occur in history as caused by God. Otherwise, we have God in league with tyrants and cancer. Rather, as Paul does in Romans 8, our

What time is it in your life? What are the opportunities God has brought to you through family, church, or personal growth that invite your attention? Talk with a trusted partner on those times, on the meanings they offer, and the peace they may bring to you and others.

task is to encourage thoughtfulness and responsiveness to the God who is able to work good through experiences and times we would not have chosen. Discerning the times is an important spiritual discipline that relies far more on faith than sight. In Greek, there are at least two words translated as "time." One, *chronos*, refers to a passage of time measured by clocks and calendars. The other, *kairos*, refers to an opportune time, the "right" time. We find meaning and peace in our lives when we tend to the moments of *kairos* God brings by the gift of God's Spirit.

CLOSING WORSHIP

Go back to the opening dialogue between Susan and James and their pastor. In what ways has this session given you insight into what is at stake for this family and what their pastor seeks for them to consider in their decision? Join hands in a prayer circle. Each individual who is comfortable doing so may offer a brief word asking God's help or guidance in finding peace and meaning in life for themselves and for others. After each person prays, invite the group to respond by saying, "Christ's peace be with you, [name of person]." Close by praying the Lord's Prayer.

[1]From *The Interpreter's Dictionary of the Bible,* Vol. 4 (Abingdon Press, 1976); page 746; and *The New Interpreter's Bible,* Vol. V (Abingdon Press, 1995); pages 278-80.

Session 6

TRUST IN GOD LEADS TO TRUE WISDOM

Proverbs 2–3; 8–9

Many people seek guidance that will help them successfully navigate life. Where can we find the guidance we need? According to Proverbs, wisdom comes as we acknowledge and trust in God with all our heart.

GATHERING

Welcome one another to the gathering. Name an individual whom you consider to be wise. Identify what wisdom that individual has taught you about life and how that has shaped you. Read aloud Proverbs 3:13-18 with that individual in mind. Offer a silent prayer of thanks for that person and the wisdom brought to you. Pray together the following prayer: Wise and wondrous God, be with us in this time together. Guide us in our thoughts and words about wisdom and of its source in you. In Jesus Christ. Amen.

Searching for Wisdom

Retreat Leader: I'd like to welcome you to the retreat house. Our time together this weekend is meant to open our hearts to the presence of God in a time and place apart. You have each chosen to join this small-group retreat on the search for wisdom, and we will begin by briefly sharing where that search has taken us in times past and why it brings us here now.

> *What wisdom operated in the past for these individuals, including yourself? What additional paths in search of wisdom do you see others, and yourself, having traveled? What are their appeals? What are their weaknesses?*

Participant A: As early as I can remember, I thought wisdom had to do with rising up the career ladder and making as much money as fast as I could. Well, I did all that. I threw myself into work. I put in hours on the weekends to get a leg up on others and hardly ever took a vacation, except when it took me to a place where I could make contacts. But then it started to dawn on me: My family had become strangers. I didn't know who I was outside of my work. So I came here.

Participant B: My children are everything to me; they are my life. Everything for me revolved around getting them to the games and the rehearsals and making sure they had everything they needed, if not wanted. I lived for them. Then, one by one, they left to go to school, to start their careers out of state. I had no one to take care of. I had always done for others; and then I didn't know who to do for. So I came here.

Participant C: I've got three post-graduate degrees from Ivy League schools. I've dabbled in most of the major religions, trying to learn as much as I can. I always thought I could make myself wise, but I don't feel I have any roots of my own. I have trouble making choices. For these reasons, I came here.

Participant D: *(You are Participant D. Where has your search for wisdom taken you, and how does that fit into your participation in this group?)*

SESSION 6: TRUST IN GOD LEADS TO TRUE WISDOM

The paths people travel toward wisdom are as varied as human interest and need. The scenario of the retreat above gives but a taste for ways in which individuals seek or practice wisdom for living. The appeal for principles, understandings, or personalities to guide us is nearly universal. Only the most autonomous of us might deny such a longing in our lives; but even then, someone or some experience had to instill that valuing of total independence.

The experience of wisdom that guides comes in our earliest years of development when as infants and then children we rely on parents and guardians to show us the way. Then such wisdom can be relatively simple in its direction: "Don't stick your finger in light sockets." We trust those who say such things, and we do not stick our fingers in sockets. As life gets more complicated, wisdom and its attendant guidance still rely on trust. We listen and heed those who, in one form or another, we trust whether by experience, authority, or knowledge.

How do you see trust and guidance related to wisdom? Reflect on that question in light of the example of wisdom you named in the opening.

The Book of Proverbs is a collection of writings in Hebrew Wisdom Literature. Brief sayings and longer expositions on wisdom comprise the book. The passages and excerpts from Proverbs in this session explore how these writings invite us to experience the wisdom of trusting God. Other works of wisdom in the Hebrew Scriptures include a number of the psalms along with Ecclesiastes, Song of Solomon, and Job. Whether in the form of songs or sayings, love poems, or a defiant questioning of life's unfathomed turns, these works of wisdom explore the connections between the created order, the God who fashioned all, and how we find the guidance to live faithfully.

Commenting on the Book of Proverbs in *An Introduction to the Old Testament*, Walter Brueggemann identifies these themes common to Wisdom Literature: "(1) [Wisdom] refers every aspect of life to the rule of God. (2) The God of Proverbs is the Creator God who in hidden ways has ordered the world. (3) The aim of wisdom instruction is that the young be educated to discern the world rightly. (4) The ordering of this world by the Creator makes certain choices productive of life and other choices productive of death."[1]

Think about the phrase "Wisdom is . . ." and complete the sentence with as many answers as possible. Reflect on the responses. What do they tell you about the way wisdom is usually conceived of in general?

Wisdom Is . . .

Filling in the blank at the end of the sentence "Wisdom is . . ." may not be as easy as it seems. Wisdom can mean many things. For some, it is a synonym of *intelligent*. For others, it is an attribute of age. For yet others, it has to do with an accumulation of knowledge. Yet, many people who are smart are not really wise. Many people who live for many years do not seem to have picked up a lot in the way of wisdom, while some youth seem wise beyond their years. Is wisdom really just what we know, or is it something more?

In Hebrew tradition, wisdom is not so much what one knows. The instruction to the wise is to "walk in the way of the good, / and keep to the paths of the just" (Proverbs 2:20). Wisdom may involve knowledge, but it is always knowledge intended to shape how we live and choose. Wisdom in the Hebrew Scriptures does not seem limited to one facet of our lives or relationships. Wisdom intends to permeate all that we do and say.

Wisdom Founded on Trust

The basis of wisdom is not intelligence, age, or even accumulation of experience. The basis of wisdom in Proverbs is trust. That is, wisdom comes in relationship with God, where our trust opens us to God's guidance. Perhaps that is why so much of the imagery of Proverbs revolves around the instruction of youth. To be sure, the wisdom tradition of Israel aims at instructing each new generation with the means of discerning what is right and good and then living with integrity to those values. However, it is not as if we arrive at such wisdom and discernment

Think about the phrase "Wisdom is . . ." and complete the sentence with as many answers as possible. Reflect on the responses. What do they tell you about the way wisdom is usually conceived of in general?

never more to need its insight. The search for wisdom and the disciplining of ourselves to discern and trust its source continues as long as we breathe.

Wisdom and relationship with God are woven closely together in the Hebrew Scriptures. At times, that relationship draws us into the web of community in celebration and praise, in service and fellowship. In a few moments, this guide will turn its attention to some of the ways in which wisdom seeks to guide and govern our relationship with neighbor. However, relationship with God also arises out of personal encounter. Notice the texts from Proverbs 2–3 continually return to an address of an individual ("my child . . . you"). Trust of God, the foundation of wisdom, finds exercise as you and I stand as individuals before God and open ourselves to the One who is trustworthy.

> *Find a partner. Read Proverbs 2:1-6 to one another, substituting the name of your partner for "my child" in 2:1. Listen to the text read to you as if it came from the one whom you find most trustworthy. What words stood out for you as you listened? Why? Share your thoughts with your partner. Notice the conditions emphasized by the threefold use of "if" in the passage. How easy is it for you to practice those conditions in your search for wisdom? How do each of them involve trust?*

> *If possible, find a quiet place apart from others in the group. Read silently to yourself Proverbs 3:1-6. This time, substitute your name for "my child" at the beginning of the reading. Read these words as if they were written to you in particular. Do a journaling exercise. For each verse, write a personal response to those words. Each response may be different: a prayer, a question, words that restate the verse in terms more directly to your life. With every response, reflect on how that verse addresses you with a call or reason to trust God. At the end of this time, offer a silent prayer that seeks a heart more open to trust and more receptive to wisdom.*

Putting Wisdom Into Practice

Read Proverbs 3:27-31. For each verse, suggest a contemporary situation that stands in need of this wisdom. Discuss how this would affect the parties involved and in what this wisdom could be brought to bear on this situation. If your group likes to do roleplay, work together to create roleplays that illustrate each of the verses. For example, you might read the verse and then do a "before" and "after" scene of what happens when wisdom is not practiced and what might result if it was. Spend time exploring how your congregation might better prepare you and others to practice such wisdom in your own lives at home, in church meetings, and in the community at large.

Wisdom is not just about understanding; it is about understanding how to live in the world. "In the world" places us in the midst of community. Israelite community was defined by covenant. The early stories of the Torah tell of a succession of covenants. First, there is the covenant with Noah, to whom God promises never again to destroy the earth, a covenant made not only with Noah and his family but with all of creation (Genesis 9). Then there is the covenant with Abram, where God promises an heir and land to one without either (Genesis 15). Finally, there is the covenant at Sinai, where God gave the Law to the people of Israel (Exodus 19-20). Blessings come to those who keep the Law, and warnings are issued against those who forget. The wisdom teachings of the Hebrew Scriptures carry that theme forward with strength and clarity. Proverbs 2:12-22 provides a concise view of how community and covenant sway on that linkage of deed and consequence, so it is not surprising that much of Proverbs provides instruction on how to live in the midst of community.

Wisdom as the practical conduct of our lives is not a concept or theme limited to Old Testament texts. Some persons view Jesus' Sermon on the Mount, for example, as an extended presentation of a new wisdom meant to shape our conduct as disciples. Consider, for example, the parable that closes the sermon: the houses built on rock

72

and sand. The premise of that teaching comes even before the parable begins: "Everyone then who hears these words of mine and acts on them will be like a wise man who built his house on rock. . . . And everyone who hears these words of mine and does not act on them will be like a foolish man who built his house on sand" (Matthew 7:24, 26). The Letter of James, an epistle many consider to grow directly out of Israel's wisdom tradition re-interpreted by the church, puts it even more bluntly: "But be doers of the word, and not merely hearers who deceive themselves" (James 1:22). Wisdom practices what it preaches, whether the "sermon" is love or grace, justice or compassion.

> *In times past, the church has sometimes struggled to understand how faith justified by grace can still insist on faith enacted in practice. How do you see grace and works as a balance for faith rather than opposing poles? Going back to where we started, how does wisdom's trust in God connect to wisdom's emphasis on faith lived and vice-versa?*

Finding Wisdom and Its Blessings

The Hebrew teachings of wisdom presume an order of creation permeated with the mark of wisdom. The cause and effect logic involved in some things leading to life and blessings and other things leading to death and curses presume there is something within the created order that makes for such a flow of consequence. Granted, some of the wisdom poets perceived a world that did not always act in such harmony. The experience of exile became, many argue, the impetus for the writing of Job and its seeking of justice in the midst of injustice.[2] Jesus himself once taught that the rain falls on the just and unjust alike (Matthew 5:45). Yet, in both of those cases, creation itself becomes the setting for the challenges.

Job finds responses, if not clear answers, in a whirlwind that points him back to the mysteries of creation (Job 38:1–41:34). When we encounter in the Proverbs passage an extended psalm of praise for Wisdom, we do not encounter a rival to God. We encounter, rather, the mystery of how God fashions creation. Wisdom is consistently referred

Read aloud Proverbs 8:22-31. Identify what is, and is not, affirmed about Wisdom and about God in this passage. How are the two related? What is the sense or emotion you feel after reading this text? What purpose do you find it to serve in the midst of a book about guidance for living?

Create a collage of wisdom and shalom. *Use the images of wisdom of Proverbs 3:8-18 for words and symbols as well as your own experience of the wisdom that guides you and the blessings it brings. Display the image in the worship center or wherever you will close the session with worship.*

to in Proverbs with feminine imagery. That fact ought not to be a call to arms for those who oppose feminine language in reference to God. Rather, that imagery simply poses yet another aspect of the mystery of the God whom we encounter in creation.

Finding wisdom is not only about locating wisdom in creation. Proverbs also seeks to identify and commend wisdom's blessings. Proverbs 3: 8-18 associates wisdom with blessings ranging from health and refreshment to prosperity and jewels. One can quickly see a danger in this: If I live wisely, I will be rich. I will be successful. Even the use of the term "successful" in the focus statement cautions against misunderstandings of religion that would turn it into spiritual pyramid games. Wisdom is not about the kind of affluence that saps character with a presumption of self-righteousness. Wisdom has to do with trust that understands we will be cared for and held in God's good hands. Proverbs says, "All her paths are peace." The word for "peace" is *shalom. Shalom* is not simply an absence of conflict; it is a fullness to life, a sense of knowing that we have all that we need from God's hand. That, in the end, is our true wisdom.

CLOSING WORSHIP

Call to mind what this session has generated in your mind and heart about wisdom. It might be a question, a new insight, or an old truth reinforced. Name one or two. Read aloud Psalm 8:1-4 in unison. Let these verses serve as your commission to seek wisdom. Pray silently about ways you can more deeply trust God's guidance and thus live wisely. Close by praying together the following prayer: God of all wisdom, help us to offer your wisdom to others. Draw us all closer to you. In Christ we pray. Amen.

---

[1]From *An Introduction to the Old Testament,* by Walter Brueggemann (Westminster John Knox Press, 2003); pages 307-08; 311.
[2]From *An Introduction to the Old Testament;* page 302.

Session

7

THE PATH OF INTEGRITY

Proverbs 11; 31

T his session explores ways God's wisdom can help us overcome negative traits such as pride and dishonesty. It offers a model for living in God's wisdom through the words of King Lemuel's mother.

GATHERING

Welcome one another to the gathering. Read the following quote: "Lead your life so you won't be ashamed to sell the family parrot to the town gossip." Briefly identify connections between the quote and the session title. Offer the following prayer: Holy One; be with us now in this time, in your word and Spirit, through our words and fellowship. Help us to see the gift and call of living with integrity as those whom you fashioned in your image. Through Jesus Christ. Amen.

A Return of Thanks

(The scene: a living room full of pictures of children and grandchildren, an old overstuffed couch on which sits a young man in his late twenties, while his grandmother sits in a rocking chair slightly to the side.)

Gram: It's so good to see you again. Phones are nice, but faces are better.

Phil: It has been too long. The place looks just like when I used to come over here on Sundays after church for lunch and pinochle all those years ago.

Gram: Well, thank you; but I have a feeling you didn't give up a weekend to fly here to tell me I still can keep up with the housework.

Phil: No, you're right about that. It's something more serious.

Gram: Phil, there's nothing wrong with you or the family, is there?

Phil: We're fine. I just wanted tell you something face to face. Thank you.

Gram: Thank me? For what?

Phil: For being who you are and for your steadiness. As long as I can remember, you always were someone I could depend on to tell me the truth; to set me straight, if needed; and to love me.

Gram: Oh, Phil, you're going to make an old woman cry. I didn't do anything special.

Phil: Well, maybe for the first time in my life I'm going to have to disagree with you. You've always been special, because you've always been so consistent with me—with all of us, really. You didn't just teach us how to live; you showed us. When I went through those hard times

78

> *What stands out for you in this story? Why? Where are the faith or God connections between that story and your own experience?*

in college, you were the one person who didn't back away from letting me know I was headed in the wrong direction but that you still loved me. You showed me the way by your own life. So I just needed to tell you, Gram, thank you.

"The Path of Integrity" forms an apt close to "Living in and as God's Creation." The theme evokes a consistency between who we are and who God has fashioned us to be in this world, for one another, and within our very selves. The wisdom texts of Proverbs provide ways for us to understand how life can be lived by God's guidance.

However, words alone often do not suffice as our teachers any more than faith can exist only in thought or words alone. The path of integrity calls out for words expressed in deeds and faith incarnate in human lives. So as you approach these texts and your conversations around them, remember they are not intended as abstract principles whose value is in the knowing alone. Wisdom, integrity, and God's guidance all come in our living as God's creation in the world of relationships: familial and communal, personal and institutional. There is no arena of our living that goes excluded from the need for consistency between belief and practice. What we think, say, and do are intended to be a seamless whole.

> *What joins wisdom and integrity in your mind? How might lingering issues or questions from previous sessions be addressed by "the path of integrity?"*

Wisdom and Integrity: What It Is and What It Is Not

Putting opposing principles or ideas side by side may form a helpful way of highlighting the differences between such viewpoints or practices. The whole of Proverbs 11 (and much of the remaining book) is written in just such a manner. There is no thread of narrative. Sometimes, there seems little connection between the verses that come grouped together in chapters. Instead, there is simply this listing of mostly independent couplets that relate what wisdom is and what it is not.

Just what is *integrity*? Dictionary definitions stress "adherence to a set of standards or a state of being sound and whole." In architecture, a structure is said to have integrity if and when its construction holds its parts together without breaks and flaws that might otherwise weaken the whole. What is integrity in a person? Those same ideas come into play. When our lives and values hold together in a way where one reflects and begets the other, we may be said to possess integrity. When we are as good as our word, we may be trusted as persons of integrity. Let us also not forget community. Paul's identification of the church as the body of Christ strongly suggests health results when Christ's community embodies the values and ministries of Jesus. Integrity is at stake when the world around us hears us talk of love and practice something else. Integrity in Christian community pushes us to consider whether the way we engage in the "business" of the church coincides with the gospel we have on our lips.

"Integrity" appears only once in Proverbs 11, when verse 3 contrasts it with "crookedness." The Hebrew word *tummah* only occurs elsewhere, interestingly,

Ask for two volunteers to read Proverbs 11 aloud. Ask one person to read the first half; ask the other person to read the second half. Notice how these verses pair opposites in their series of contrasts (for example, "pride" and "humble," "upright" and "treacherous," "righteousness" and "wicked"). What is the cumulative effect of these verses and their contrasts? What does it communicate about the perception and practice of wisdom in the world?

Compose a list of qualities associated with integrity. What are its synonyms? What are its evidences in our midst and the signs of its absence? Create two or three roleplay situations, individual and community based, where the outcome hinges on integrity. Do the roleplays with alternate endings, depending on whether integrity is exercised or not. Discuss what those situation raised in your mind about integrity, especially what the cost of exercising integrity can sometimes bring.

> *How does the integrity of Job compare and contrast with some of the statements about wisdom and integrity in Proverbs 11? What do Proverbs, Job, and Paul contribute to your understanding and practice of integrity?*

in the Book of Job. There, it is used by Job's wife to describe him in an ironic plea: "Do you still persist in your integrity? Curse God, and die" (Job 2:9). Even more ironically, it is the word God uses to describe Job's constancy of faith in the face of the suffering Job has endured (2:3).

At times, Proverbs might seem to leave the impression that wisdom and integrity always result in blessing. The integrity of Job raises an intriguing issue. Sometimes, it is our integrity, not our lack of it, that results in trouble. Job serves as a helpful caution against some modern theologies that espouse the wise will always and ever prosper, with the unfortunate implication that evil times fall only on those who deserve and bring them on themselves. Integrity is not an inoculation against trouble. Integrity allows us to maintain our identity and vocation with consistency in the face of good or ill and not be changed by outward fortune. Such integrity takes shape in later words of wisdom offered by Paul: "I know what it is to have little, and I know what it is to have plenty. In any and all circumstances I have learned the secret. . . . I can do all things through him who strengthens me" (Philippians 4:12, 13). For the Christian, to live in Christ is to live with integrity.

Integrity and Community

While integrity may rely on the exercise of individual character and choice, the wisdom of Proverbs insists that its fruits spill out into the life of community. Several sets of verses from the two chapters of Proverbs explored in this session reveal that truth and intent.

> *Read Proverbs 11:1, 9-14 and 31:8-9. How do these Scriptures speak to you about the connections between individual integrity and its effects on the community?*

There is, first of all, a strong link in these chapters between wisdom and matters of justice and compassion. Justice looms large in the opening verse that

81

contrasts false balances and accurate weights. By means of inaccurate weights, a merchant could easily take advantage of a customer. Amos 8:5 lists this among the abuses that brought down God's judgment against Israel. It is not coincidental that the following verse makes mention of abuse of the poor. The rich might have recourse against those who corrupted trade in that fashion; the poor would not. Rarely does injustice take down persons of means and power in the stories of

Identify one or two situations in your community and/or the wider world in which the poor go abused today. Reflect on the verses you have read from Proverbs 11 and 31, along with 14:31. What is the wisdom they bring to those situations, and to the meaning and calling to live as God's creation in creation? How might our living with integrity to that calling bring good news and justice to the poor in those situations? What are some practical actions you as a group might take in response to those situations?

Scripture. That truth holds true today. Dishonesty, a lack of integrity in business and relationship with neighbor, still takes a heavier toll on those with less resources to challenge. Proverbs has numerous references elsewhere that warn against taking advantage of the poor (22:22). The underlying principle for such teachings is given graphic statement in Proverbs 14:31: "Those who oppress the poor insult their Maker, / but those who are kind to the needy honor [God]." Doing justice is not simply the humane thing to do; it is the godly thing to do. For in the wisdom of proverbs, justice and integrity are cut from the same cloth.

Compassion deepens justice with acts of human kindness. It is possible to work for justice for oppressed people without any real inclination to spending time with the "clientele." Compassion prevents such ministry from devolving into pity. Compassion brings human touch and concern into the equation. In a portion of the song of praise for the capable wife in Chapter 31, the writer mentions her concern and action for the poor; but notice how that image is framed: "She opens her hand to the poor, and reaches out her hands to the needy" (31: 20). Can you see such hands in action, opening to another's need, reaching out in hopes of touching or lifting or stroking another into life? There is risk, of course.

Think for a moment when you have touched another person in need or have been touched when you have been in need. How did it feel to offer touch or to receive touch? Discuss your experience with a partner. What ministries in your congregation, existing or potential, involve hand-to-hand contact? Consider becoming a participant in that ministry – remembering that integrity is not only the wholeness between word and deed but integrity can also mean the wholeness between our words toward and our touch of others.

Hands can get dirty. Hands can feel pain. Hands bring you into contact with another in a way that words cannot.

The writer praises this woman's hands-on ministry to people in need, and there is deep wisdom in that praise. Our hands are an extension of our selves. To act and live with integrity, in terms of touching another's life, means extending more than good wishes or sending money on its way. It means extending the gift and taking the risk of touching another with our very selves.

A Song of Wisdom Incarnate

In Session 2, the comments on Psalm 145 included a brief explanation of a form of poetry called "acrostic," where each verse or line is a successive letter of the alphabet. In Proverbs 31, we once again encounter an acrostic work. One of the reasons acrostics were used, besides a memory device in an oral tradition, was to express in a poem's structure the theme of completeness or wholeness. "From A to Z" would be a modern expression of what an acrostic seeks to convey. Proverbs 31:20-31 intends to express the gifts of a woman whose works and capabilities are so inclusive, so each verse begins with a different letter of the alphabet.

The words are attributed to the words taught to a certain King Lemuel by his mother in 31:1. Though the name and figure is unknown to us, that does not matter. The focus in this work is on a woman who has translated the call of wisdom and the path of integrity into her conduct of life. The fact that we do not know her name may be quite intentional on the part of the author. It leaves open the possibility to fill in another's name, even our own, simply yet profoundly by living with such wisdom.

For some, the words and imagery of this poem may seem, at least on the surface, a bit lim-

> *Read aloud Proverbs 31:10-31. Discuss the variety of reasons why she is praised here. How would such wisdom take shape in women and men today?*

iting, as if wisdom for women must always be experienced and expressed in terms of relationship with husband and children. The poem goes deeper than that, though. The poem praises a woman who has exercised strength in relationship and acumen in economies. Some recent interpreters have reflected on this in terms of the experience of Judaism in the exile. Persian sources indicate men there sought out women who could be trusted to handle the affairs of business and home economies, much as this poem extols those public roles. Some of the verses use language and imagery usually in praise of men (the warrior image of verse 17 or the purchasing and working of land in verse 16). This is a poem that breaks, not reinforces, stereotypes imposed by gender.[1]

It is a poem in praise of one who has embodied wisdom and made integrity incarnate in the routine of life. I have heard, and on occasion, read this poem at funerals and memorial services. The individuals and families who made that request experienced such gifts in the person they gathered to remember. The poem can serve that purpose; but even more importantly, it can serve the two-fold purpose of calling to remembrance for praise those who have served as our mentors in wisdom and summon our own enactment of integrity. Wisdom always seeks to influence more than our understanding of life; it seeks to transform our practice of living. We find in others the embodiment of wisdom, much as this writer found in the words

> *Think now of the person whose wisdom has most influenced you in life. Write in a journal entry an acrostic in praise of that individual. You may not have time in this session to do a complete acrostic in English (26 lines, one for each letter of the alphabet), but work on what you can now. At some time during the coming week, add lines as you are able. Do not feel forced, but grow out of what you have gained from the person you are writing about.*

84

of Lemuel's mother an apt conclusion to a book devoted to wisdom. When we do, it behooves us to speak in praise of those who show us the way to live as God's creation in creation, in praise of God, and in praise of that individual.

The previous paragraph spoke of a two-fold remembrance, the second being this poem's evoking of our own enactment of wisdom. Whether you are aware of it, you likely serve for at least one other person as a potential source of wisdom and integrity. The calling to be wise does not belong to the intellectual or religious elite. It belongs to us all. The Book of Proverbs stands opened to the whole church to give guidance on what it means to walk with integrity and live with wisdom. Wisdom is calling, and it is calling you. Will you follow?

CLOSING WORSHIP

Gather in a circle, and join hands. Thank one another for the time you have shared and energy that has been devoted and the wisdom that has been brought in one another's perspectives. Underscore the final two lines in the previous paragraph. The wisdom of living in and as God's creation becomes our commission together. Unite in these closing words: God of the journey, we thank you that we live in and as your creation. Open us to your way. Grant us your Spirit to guide us, draw us into community that refreshes us, and deepen our trust through service. In Jesus Christ. Amen.

[1]From *Introduction to the Old Testament;* pages 315-16.

Appendix

Background Scriptures for
"Creation: Living in and as God's Creation"

Psalm 8	Mark 16
Psalm 104	Ecclesiastes 1:1-11
Psalm 139	Ecclesiastes 3
Psalm 145	Proverbs 2–3
Job 1–3	Proverbs 8–9
Job 114	Proverbs 11
Job 38:1-4, 16-17	Proverbs 31
Job 42:1-6	

The Committee on the Uniform Series

The Committee on the Uniform Series (CUS) is made up of persons appointed by their respective denominations, which, although differing in certain elements of faith and polity, hold a common faith in Jesus Christ, the Son of God, as Lord and Savior, whose saving gospel is to be taught to all humankind. CUS has about 70 members who represent 19 Protestant denominations in the US and Canada, who work together to develop the International Bible Lessons for Christian Teaching. A team from this committee develops the cycles of Scriptures and themes that form the backbone of the Bible lesson development guides. The cycles present a balance between Old and New Testaments, although the weight is on the latter. Cycles through 2016 are organized around the following themes: creation, call, covenant, Christ, community, commitment, God, hope, worship, tradition, faith, and justice.

—MARVIN CROPSEY,
Chair, Committee on the Uniform Series